Praise for D███ D1245760

"*Dear Department Chair* is a welcomed collection that builds on the tradition of 'lifting as we climb.' Kudos to the editors who took it upon themselves to offer a readable collection about leadership in the academy. Colleagues, both women and men, of all hues will learn something from this work. I wish that it had been available when I became chair!"

—Joye Bowman, Senior Associate Dean, College of Humanities and Fine Arts, University of Massachusetts Amherst

"Indeed, this important collection gives voice to a truth known to some but ignored by too many: If you look closely, Black women leaders are either present or in the process of being made. A must read for upper administrators, mentors, allies, and leaders in the making."

—Tara T. Green, PhD, Chair and CLASS Distinguished Professor of African American Studies, University of Houston

"While there are many books about academic administrators, this unique and inspirational volume is the very first to center the perspectives and experiences of Black women leaders in academia. Desperately needed and long overdue, it is full of sage advice and concrete strategies for success, encouraging self-reflection, wellness, and humility; and emphasizing sisterhood, peer mentorship, and collaboration. It should be required reading for all academic leaders!"

—Yolanda Covington-Ward, professor and Chair, W. E. B. Du Bois Department of Afro-American Studies, University of Massachusetts Amherst

"Exemplifying a key maxim in Black women's survival and achievement, 'lifting as we climb,' this collection demonstrates to sister-scholar administrators and their non-Black colleagues that collaboration, commiseration, and celebration are strategic tools, meaningful service, and sources of strength for Black women leaders in higher education today. These thought-provoking essays are essential reading for all who seek to create academic excellence that is both inclusive and humane."

—Bonnie Thornton Dill, University of Maryland

Dear Department Chair

Dear Department Chair

Letters from Black Women Leaders to the Next Generation

Edited by Stephanie Y. Evans,
Stephanie Shonekan, and
Stephanie G. Adams

Foreword by Dr. Johnnetta Betsch Cole

WAYNE STATE UNIVERSITY PRESS
DETROIT

ISBN 9780814350744 (paperback)
ISBN 9780814350751 (e-book)

Library of Congress Control Number: 2022951628

Cover illustration and design by Kristle Marshall.

Wayne State University Press rests on Waawiyaataanong, also referred to
as Detroit, the ancestral and contemporary homeland of the Three Fires
Confederacy. These sovereign lands were granted by the Ojibwe, Odawa,
Potawatomi, and Wyandot Nations, in 1807, through the Treaty of
Detroit. Wayne State University Press affirms Indigenous sovereignty and
honors all tribes with a connection to Detroit. With our Native neighbors,
the press works to advance educational equity and promote a better future
for the earth and all people.

Wayne State University Press
Leonard N. Simons Building
4809 Woodward Avenue
Detroit, Michigan 48201-1309

Visit us online at wsupress.wayne.edu.

Contents

Acknowledgments   vii

Foreword: A Letter from Dr. Johnnetta Betsch Cole,
President Emerita, Spelman College and
Bennett College   ix

Introduction: A Letter from the Three Dr. Stephanies:
On the Path to Wellness, Academic Sisterhood,
and Focus   1
Stephanie Y. Evans, Stephanie Shonekan, and Stephanie G. Adams

    Department Chair Job Description   35

Part 1 Letters from the Chair

1. A Chair's Epistle: Finding the Color Purple and
    Your Leadership Identity in a Field of Email   43
    Tiffany Gilbert

2. From Freedom to Liberty: I Am Not My Skin   57
    April Langley

3. Sisterhood Beyond Scholarship: Advice to
    a New Sister-Director   71
    Janaka B. Lewis

4. Leadership at the Community College: Supporting and
    Celebrating the Diversity of Community   79
    Sandra Jowers-Barber

5. "Holding Sheshelf Together": Citizenship of Feelings
    and Living Your Sacred Self   91
    Julia S. Jordan-Zachery

6. Dear Dean: Some Suggestions for Mentoring
Black Women in the Academy   101
Régine Michelle Jean-Charles

Part II Letters from Upper Administration

7. How and When I Enter: Pearls of Wisdom for
Courageous Leadership in the Academy   111
Carol E. Henderson

8. Lift as We Climb and When We Get
There, Mentor Others   119
Theresa Rajack-Talley

9. Hear My Prayer: Embrace the Possibilities of
Leadership with Humility   135
Colette M. Taylor

10. Pulling the Table to My Chair at EMU   147
Eunice Myles Jeffries

*Afterword: A Letter from Dr. Tracy
Sharpley-Whiting, Co-Chair of Chair at
the Table Project, Vice Provost for Arts and
Libraries, Vanderbilt University*   157

Contributor Bios   161

Index   169

Acknowledgments

Stephanie Evans thanks Dr. Sharpley-Whiting for graciously accepting my invitation to co-lead the Chair at the Table project and to be an *active* partner in seeing the project to fruition. Tracy, I'm not only grateful for your willingness to show that academic sisterhood is a verb, I'm inspired by the love and kindness that you center in all of your work. Thank you for levying your esteemed name, established network, and considerable resources to grow the Black women's chair network into a dynamic system of collective care. Thank you to Drs. Shonekan and Adams for emphasizing that serious work can be fun and meaningful and that the National Association of Colored Women's motto, "lifting as we climb," is a living model of Black women's work. Thanks also to Dr. Rhonda Williams, who recommended I reach out to our beloved colleague to expand the reach of this chair's network. I remain grateful to my mentors, especially John H. Bracey, Jr. and Esther Terry who, when I was a PhD student, chaired the W. E. B. Du Bois Department at the University of Massachusetts Amherst in a spirit of service. As always, I'm thankful to my husband, Dr. Curtis Byrd, who is not only the love of my life but a constant reminder of what a blessing it is to have a life partner on this life journey and the joy possible in the struggle for health and wellness.

Stephanie Shonekan thanks my namesakes (Evans and Adams) for letting me ride with them on this editorial journey. Deep gratitude to my mentors—Camilla Williams (RIP), Portia K. Maultsby, Lisa Brock, Joye Bowman, Cheryl Johnson-Odim, April Langley, and Bonnie Thornton Dill—all Black women who understand what it is like to be in my shoes, and have lavished me with wisdom, time, and energy over the years. Also grateful for other mentors who have been in my corner, including Pat Okker, Cooper Drury, Fernando Orejuela, Adam Seagrave, and David Krause. Big hugs to my sister-scholars—Sheri-Marie Harrison, Keona Ervin, and Cristina Mislan. Lots of love to my very own people—Richard, Alison,

Tomiwa, Faramola, Ojurere, and Mojuba. And so much love and gratitude to my heavenly angels, Martin and Mummy.

Stephanie Adams thanks Dr. Stephanie Y. Evans for inviting me to join the Department Chair Collaborative in 2019 and including me in this current project, which will change the way higher education sees Black women leaders. I thank Dr. Stephanie Shonekan for her authenticity and sisterhood. Thanks to my mentor and Shero, Dr. Johnnetta Betsch Cole, for a beautifully written foreword to this work. You have been a guide and mentor to so many, and I am humbled to be one of them. I have learned so much from you about what it means to be a Black woman leader. I am because of YOU!!! Thanks to my parents, Drs. Howard and Eloise Adams, for their example, guidance, continued support, and unconditional love. Lastly, to my wife, Sandra T. H. Adams, thanks for being the glue that keeps our family going.

The Three Stephanies editorial team thanks Stephanie Williams and the entire Wayne State University Press team for championing this project. Williams, we were excited to work with you, of course, not only because you are a Stephanie but because you represent the best of what this collection stands for. As the first Black woman head of a university press, it was fitting that you identified this project as a good fit as a cornerstone of your legacy. We are fortunate that our network includes Shonekon, who proposed WSUP as the best fit, despite several other very good options. Your enthusiasm and commitment made it clear this was the best home for our work. Thank you for all you have done to support this project. We are also grateful to the WSUP team, especially acquisitions editor Sandra Korn, for facilitating the publication process with ease and grace, as well as Polly Rosenwaike for her editorial expertise. Team Stephanie is especially grateful for the indexing services of our esteemed colleague Dr. Janet Sims-Wood—your attention to detail and offering your expertise to our project is much appreciated.

Foreword

A Letter from Dr. Johnnetta Betsch Cole, President Emerita, Spelman College and Bennett College

Dear Department Chair, Director, Dean, Provost, President, and other Higher Education Administrators,

When my mentee, colleague, and sister-friend Dr. Stephanie Adams asked on behalf of herself and Drs. Stephanie Evans and Stephanie Shonekan if I would write a letter to each of you, I immediately said that I would do so. Of course, I would need to read the letters from each of the three Dr. Stephanies, and the additional ten letters that are the body of this book. I looked forward to doing so, knowing that these letters would echo many of my own experiences as the Founding Director of the Black Studies Program at Washington State University; Associate Provost for Undergraduate Education at the University of Massachusetts Amherst; Director of Latin American and Caribbean Studies at the City University of New York; and President of Spelman College and Bennett College. However, because I was in those positions many years ago, I knew that in these letters I would read about challenges that are very specific to what today's Black women administrators must wrestle with because of recent racial reckonings, the surge in white supremacist ideology, attacks on women's rights for abortions, and a rise in far-right politics across the United States and the world.

I also accepted the invitation to write this letter because it would put me in touch with every Black woman academic administrator who will read this book. Thus, I would not only connect with women academic administrators whose lived experiences are like many of my own, I would also connect with Black women academic administrators who are much younger than I—women who are future leaders of American colleges and universities.

This book is a highly valuable resource for the next generation of academic leaders. It is filled with information based on lived experiences of Black women who are currently administrators. And the sharing of those lived experiences is buttressed with specific data. There is an African proverb that says: "Until the lion tells the story of the hunt, the story will always glorify the hunter." To make an important point, I want to add my proverb: "Until the lioness tells the story of the hunt, you haven't heard all of the stories."

Whether you are in your first year as an academic administrator or you have years of experience in this arena, there is much for you to learn from and to be inspired and fortified by in these letters from our sister-colleagues. Of course, no matter where one is on the ladder of academic administration, many benefits come from learning from others, and each of us has the responsibility to share what we know. As another African proverb says: "She who learns must teach, and she who teaches must learn."

While the letters in this volume chronicle many similarities across Black women academic administrators' experiences, a diversity of experiences is also represented here. Race and gender identities strongly affect how Black women administrators are responded to in the academy, but race and gender are only two of the multiple identities that can influence how Black women fare in top-level jobs at colleges and universities. In addition to experiencing discrimination based on their race and gender, Black women in academic leadership roles also suffer discrimination based on age, sexual orientation, religion, and disabilities. As I like to quip: If you have seen one Black woman, you haven't seen us all!

For African American women, as indeed for individuals from all marginalized communities, as well as individuals with privilege from their white skin and/or economic status, the type of school where they work will be a factor in their experiences as an administrator. Historically Black Colleges and Universities (HBCUs) have notable differences from Predominately White Institutions. There are similarities but also differences between HBCUs and Hispanic-Serving Institutions. Tribal colleges share some attributes with these two kinds of academic communities while also possessing distinct characteristics of their own. And of course, a woman who is a Black academic administrator may well have very different experiences in a small liberal arts college than in a large research institution.

This book is filled with sage advice, the kind of counsel I wish I had received when I was transitioning from my role as a professor to an academic administrator. At the risk of being repetitive, and without claiming to have THE list of what every Black woman should do to be a successful academic administrator, I want to contribute seven of the many lessons I have learned on my journey in the world of higher education administration.

Lesson One

Counsel I was given when I was a youngster growing up in the South during the Jim Crow era is advice that countless Black parents continue to give their children. Namely, you must be twice as good to get half as far as White folks. Today, even with progress in race relations since the days of Jim Crow, Black parents still caution their children to be "extra prepared" for any task if they wish to be successful. Having learned this lesson as a youngster certainly helped me to do well in school and to follow my years in the professorate with positions in academic administration.

Lesson Two

During the 1960s, when I was the founding director of one of the first Black Studies programs in our country, I learned how to own my power while leading with humility. A group of faculty and students and I found success in initiating a Black Studies program and in increasing the number of Black faculty and students on campus, even as I came to appreciate that there is no contradiction in owning one's power to be a change agent while also remaining humble.

Lesson Three

In each of the administrative roles that I have served in within the academy, I have seen the benefits of a collaborative style of leadership.

This way of getting work done is captured in the African proverb "If you want to go fast, go alone. If you want to go far, go together."

Lesson Four

Throughout my years in academic administration, I repeatedly witnessed what young folks now call "Black girl magic." That is the ability of Black women administrators to "make do when don't wants to prevail"; to create successful programs when the prevailing view is that it cannot be done; to mentor a younger colleague so that she begins to soar to the height of her possibilities; and to inspire students to accept the truth in these words of Liberian President Ellen Johnson Sirleaf: "If your dreams do not scare you, they are not big enough." I learned the importance of thinking and planning on a grand scale, and then putting in the time and effort to make those plans happen.

Lesson Five

During every period when I assumed a role as an academic leader, I sought out and developed a strong circle of sisterly support. Such support included informal networks of Black women in similar positions. Sometimes it was just a matter of being on the other end of a phone call with a sister-scholar or sister-administrator who would pose a question I needed to respond to, or who would be a listening ear as I worked through a complex issue or concern.

Lesson Six

Several letters in this volume emphasize the importance of self-care. This is a lesson I wish I had learned much earlier in my career in the academy. But better late than never. Audre Lorde put it succinctly: "Caring for myself is not self-indulgence. It is self-preservation, and that is an act of political warfare."

Lesson Seven

During the years when I was an academic administrator, I learned the importance of getting passionate about the work that must be done and taking pleasure in doing it well. Serving as a Black woman administrator in a college or university is a very challenging job, a job that in my opinion cannot be done well unless one finds joy in doing it. These words of Dr. Maya Angelou speak to this point: "You can only become truly accomplished at something you love. Don't make money your goal. Instead, pursue the things you love doing and then do them so well that people can't take their eyes off of you."

Onward!
Johnnetta Betsch Cole

Introduction

A Letter from the Three Dr. Stephanies

On the Path to Wellness, Academic Sisterhood, and Focus

STEPHANIE Y. EVANS
Professor, Georgia State University

STEPHANIE SHONEKAN
Dean, University of Maryland, College Park

STEPHANIE G. ADAMS
Dean, University of Texas at Dallas

Dear Department Chair, Director, Dean, Provost, President, and other Higher Education Administrators:

Thank you for joining this discussion! "Thank you" is a phrase you may hear rarely in your administrative position. Having been in some of the roles you now hold, we want to start by saying thank you for caring enough to do this work. Thank you for seeking ways to sustain yourself in this work. Thank you for searching for resources that improve your work in order to more effectively support those in your academic areas. Thank you for joining the discussion about how to make academic administrative work more humane and to help institutionalize ways of wellness, excellence, and equity.

As evidenced by the December 2022 announcement of Professor Claudine Gay as the new President of Harvard University, Black women are making their way up the leadership ladder in higher education. As a former Dean of Social Sciences and of Arts and Sciences, Dr. Gay had the institutional leadership experience to prepare her for a top post. As we, a new generation of Black women, prepare ourselves for leadership, understanding personal and professional pressures can increase our sustainability and efficacy. This collection of letters offers an opportunity to reflect and learn in community.

The appointment of Professor Gay is noteworthy for several reasons, including its historical importance and Harvard's responding to the need for diverse representation in leadership. Representation is not only about cultural identity but also about excellence that can happen when diverse experiences, viewpoints, and areas of expertise are brought to the table. Most importantly, representation is about commitment to acknowledge the barriers that still exist, the sacrifices of those who came before us, and a commitment to ensure greater access to the Ivory Tower.

Higher education is facing many challenges, including how to value people over profit, how to deal with structural and cultural inequities that have deep historical roots, and how to help the next generation move the nation and the world beyond normalizing hate, violence, and exploitation. Representation does not always guarantee moves toward equity, but we should remain hopeful. President Gay will need strength for her journey to do hard work with joy. It is possible to make necessary campus changes in the spirit of progressive leaders from Mary McLeod Bethune to Ruth Simmons (and to honor the critical traditions of Anna Julia Cooper and W. E. B. Du Bois), though it won't be easy. *Dear Department Chair* puts institutional leadership in context and offers advice about how to keep administrative duties in perspective.

Regardless of your heritage, background, or identity, we hope viewing higher education through the multidimensional lens of Black women administrators will improve your leadership vision. Welcome to this ongoing conversation about the future of academic leadership. We have facilitated this forum to recognize the challenges you face. We offer our experiences as tools for perspective as you locate possible solutions to problems you will most likely encounter.

Origins of This Work: Chair at the Table Network

This volume emerged from Chair at the Table, a research collective established in spring 2018 as a peer-mentoring network. Members of the network are current and former Black women department chairs at colleges and universities across the US and Canada. This research collective considers Black women's perspectives of academic leadership, particularly in light of recent 50th anniversary commemorations of the establishment of Black Studies and Women's Studies.

A multitude of issues are discussed in the Chair at the Table gatherings. For example, the mentoring workshop held on January 8, 2021, addressed a series of questions on several themes, which we grouped into four categories:

1. Administration 101
2. Leadership, Balance, and Self-Development
3. DEI, Change, and Transformation
4. The People: Faculty, Staff, Students, and Community

The lists we developed for each category, enumerated below, reference some of the substantial issues, tasks, and questions that this book aims to consider.

Issues on the Table

Administration 101

- Journey to current role / trials and accomplishments (panelist experiences)
- Charting a path from tenure to chair / CV analysis
- How does one prepare to become chair? Dean? / Paths toward administrative positions / Advancing from chair to dean
- When and why to shift from faculty to admin positions
- Advice for early career faculty considering administration and leadership positions / How to decide if administration is right for you

- Benefits of doing administrative work
- Chair duties
- Fundraising and program building
- Budget management
- Negotiating to obtain resources
- Programming best practices
- Best practices for mentoring and succession planning
- Transitioning from chair to higher-level positions
- Managing personalities and conflicts / Managing resistance
- Advocating for department / Managing department or university conflict
- Crisis management
- Helping unit survive when college is moving in different direction
- Establishing sponsors
- Building buy-in / Building support networks in and outside of your department
- Ways to obtain the correct roles to lead to higher ed positions
- What to do after chair
- How to thrive and be innovative as dean
- Transitioning from associate dean role to administrative role (i.e., President of Diversity, Equity, and Inclusion, Director of Teaching and Learning, or Vice President for Faculty Development)
- Renegotiating salaries / Promotion negotiations with chair position
- Better negotiating and acquisition of resources
- Navigating department politics / How to navigate the politics of higher administration
- Navigating changing and challenging political landscapes
- Flexibility in the age of COVID–19

Leadership, Balance, and Self-Development
- Expectations / Strategies for success
- How to adjust to being chair for the first time

- Making the most of the position
- How to leverage current work for the future / Professional development
- Time balance or how to maintain a research agenda / Book completion
- Managing administration with teaching and research
- Workload / Balancing invisible labor
- Work-research-personal life balance
- Daily workflow and time management / Time management techniques
- How to shift from the pre-tenure "no" to a post-tenure/ midcareer "yes" without getting overwhelmed by the shift in load and responsibilities
- Family dynamics
- Navigating work relationships—getting personal enough but having boundaries
- Transitioning from faculty to leadership
- Reflections: real life challenges, successes, and overcoming moments
- Mentorship, collaboration, and publishing
- Skill development and specialized training
- Knowing when to leave the position for self-preservation and/or principles
- Thoughts on the status of academia and changing landscape (pre- and post-COVID-19)
- Building a space that leaves the door open for others to walk through / At what point do we get rid of the table?
- Mentorship vs. sponsorship
- Building networks
- How to be heard
- Maintaining your identity
- How to build your "squad" of other women who can support and encourage you, especially if you don't have one or have never built one
- Protecting your intellectual property
- Scholarships / Fellowships / Grants to support educational and career advancement

- Returning to classroom
- Building community off campus

DEI, *Change, and Transformation*
- Positionality of Black women leaders at PWIs
- HBCUs and the patriarchy / Chairing at HBCUs / Chairing at HBCU as a minority
- Navigating through the academy's racism / Dismantling racism
- Dealing with sexism / Mansplaining
- Dealing with microaggressions / Whitesplaining
- How to not be a token at the table / Navigation of tokenism in leadership positions
- Black women in leadership positions / Developing mentoring / Grooming relationships with women in leadership or administrative positions
- Being the "only" or one of few as both unit administrator and faculty / Being the first—and often only—BIPOC woman in the room
- Leading a racially homogeneous department
- Building real alliances
- Higher ed leadership among women of color in the digital age
- Leveraging power for equity, managing DEI in curriculum with instructors
- RCM [responsibility-centered management] / Making effective and transformative change
- Race and gender politics
- Leading humanities-based programs in STEM forward settings
- How to insure we advance racial justice and Black well-being from our positions of power and influence
- Navigating the "what about me" resistance to equity issues
- How to be chair as a woman and an immigrant in a department with strong male personalities / How to make DEI a priority for the department and the college

- How to remain true to racial justice and do your job
- Navigating these upper echelons as a Black woman
- How to lead authentically while juggling various duties and others' interpretations of those identities

The People: Faculty, Staff, Students, and Community
- Supervising faculty
- Supporting faculty during COVID-19
- Working with challenging faculty
- Protecting and mentoring junior Black faculty / Creating mentoring programs for faculty
- BIPOC faculty hiring, promotion, and retention
- Navigating resistant faculty
- Retaining faculty
- Mentoring junior faculty / Mentoring students
- Developing leadership pipelines for BIPOC faculty
- Higher ed leadership advancement among lecturers vs. T/TT faculty
- Effectively supporting and advocating for Black and Brown faculty across all ranks
- Pipeline potential for postdocs
- What do you do when you don't have an administrative assistant and if you are treated like one?
- Navigating student activism
- How to leverage our higher education positions for influence in the wider society, whether in media, government, or other spaces of influence
- Leveraging chair experience beyond the department
- Chair activism
- Transferrable skills

Foundational Reading on Black Women and Leadership

Some of the items in the detailed list above are rooted in earlier discussions. For example, conference panels held during a 2019 symposium, sponsored by Dr. Tracy Sharpley-Whiting at Vanderbilt

University, have been published in *Palimpsest* (SUNY Press, Volume 10, issue 2, 2021) under the title *Chair at the Table: Black Women and Academic Leadership—Reflections and Recommendations*. The Table of Contents includes the following:

Editor Introduction:
    Tracy Sharpley-Whiting
Guest Editor Introduction:
    "We've Been Lovers on a Mission"
    Stephanie Y. Evans
All Eyez on Me: On Being Black, Female, and a First-Gen Leader in the Academy
    Carol E. Henderson
A Real-World Discourse on Intellectual Identity, Thought Leadership, and the Black Woman Academic Chair
    Katherine Bankole-Medina
The Black Woman Chair in a Burning Building
    Michelle R. Dunlap
Reflections of a Former Department Chair: A Path to University Service and Leadership Skills
    Janice L. Sumler-Edmond
Chairing as Self-Care: Strategies for Combatting the Cultural Identity Taxation Trap for Black Women Chairs
    Donna J. Nicol
Being One of the Chosen: Making Space for Students at the Table
    Tara T. Green
The Job I Never Wanted Was Exactly What I Needed
    Stephanie G. Adams
We Do Not Have to Be White or Men to Lead: Redefining and Assessing Black Women's Leadership
    Theresa Ann Rajack-Talley

Building on these and other themes, the letters in this book unpack assumptions about the role of chair and upper administrators, with a specific point of reference to ongoing Diversity, Equity, and Inclusion efforts. These letters offer contrasting reflections of diverse experiences based on institution type, academic discipline, interactions with university committees, personal backgrounds, professional goals, and intellectual trajectories.

In both the *Palimpsest* journal and the present collection, authors supply context for best practices and provide specific advice about how to manage time, expectations, and inevitable issues with people, institutions, and environmental factors. The work of the Chair at the Table research collective provides tools for faculty interested in administrative experience, mentoring guides for current chairs, resources for those moving "Beyond the Chair," and reference points for upper-level administrators who are working to diversify their ranks in ways that move beyond tokenism of one or two figures who agree to maintain the status quo.

Letters from the Chair: Three Dr. Stephanies and a Collection of Epistles for Future Leaders

The co-editors of this book have much in common but also offer our unique perspectives. We are Stephanie Evans (humanities and social science), Stephanie Shonekan (humanities and arts), and Stephanie Adams (engineering). We were drawn together not simply because we share a name but because we share a vision. As we got to know each other in professional development spaces, we recognized how our experiences as academic administrators brought us together in community. While discussing our time in "the chair" and beyond, we began to share the pressure points of our administrative work and strategize to address them—together. We are part of a growing network of scholar-administrators committed to sharing our insights to support the future development of Black women administrators, in particular, and to present opportunities for others to support this growing demographic.

Dear Department Chair serves as a scaffolding for those currently in (or considering) the position of chair, director, dean, provost, president, or other leadership positions. The department chair has always been "the hot seat," but amidst a global pandemic, political chaos, racial uprisings, a rollback of women's rights, and outright attacks on academic freedom, we know too well the stress encountered by academic leadership.

This book of letters—in the epistolary tradition—was written to directly address an audience of Black women administrators, as well as mentors, supervisors, colleagues, and campus community members who support us. In her essay "Letters to Our Daughters: Black Women's Memoirs as Epistles of Human Rights, Healing, and Inner Peace," published in *The Black Intellectual Tradition: African American Thought in the Twentieth Century* (2021), Stephanie Evans traces the ancient history of epistles and letter writing in Hebrew, Egyptian, Ethiopian, Chinese, English, and other cultures. For Black women, life writing is a form of intergenerational communication, as Evans explains:

> Epistolary writing is widely recognized to mean letters or documents written as correspondence. These letters may be published or not, but epistles are, in an ancient form, prose of communication, as can be seen in some biblical verse. . . . Memoirs are mentors. . . . Empowerment through literature can be a multigenerational experience . . . I read Africana memoirs as collected letters, documents, and missives written to pass on wisdom. Even when narratives are not explicit about the audiences they address, many readers are clear about how they read life stories for more than comprehension; they read for evaluation and application. They read and can be changed. (Evans 2021, 100–108)

We hope administrators who engage in this conversation about department chairs and other leadership posts read these letters and are changed. Specifically, we hope to change the "top-down" nature of administration that is primarily based on hierarchy, punishment, manufactured austerity, and accumulation of power at top levels, without properly valuing those individuals—like faculty, staff, and department chairs—who provide the central services to students and the university community. We hope those changes are then reflected in the culture and systems of academe nationwide and globally.

Letters in this volume come from Black women administrators who seek to unveil the unique positionality of race, gender, and unit leadership. The letter-as-essay form makes transparent the intended primary audience, while, as a public document, it offers an opportunity for others to witness and learn from authors who offer intimate reflections on their life work. This book features experiences from department chairs, directors, deans, provosts, presidents, and other administrators as a critical and transformative analysis of race, gender, and higher education leadership. As experienced administrators in a variety of academic disciplines, we offer reflections and recommendations, penned in the form of letters to the next generation of academic leaders, as a resource to redefine the academy. We hope to demystify traditional posts as well as shed light on scholarly societies and professional organization leadership.

The dozens of scholars in the Chair at the Table network have decades of experience at various institution types. Representative leaders from the network come together in this volume to collectively suggest a paradigm shift for unit heads in higher education. Whether an administrative faculty is called chair, head, or director, or is considered to be higher on the academic ladder, leadership experience is shared here for the benefit of all. Inspired by Solange's "Seat at the Table" and "Borderline (An Ode to Self Care)," this collective aspires to "make less war" inside and outside the walls of academe.

Our imagined community of readers includes the following:

- all new academic department chairs and deans
- women of color in leadership positions or those interested in future opportunities
- current higher education administration seeking to diversify their campus leadership team
- students, faculty, and administrators in university higher education programs
- administrators in positions related or adjacent to research and higher education (law, business, medicine and public health, nonprofit, museums, etc.)

In this volume, letters begin with "Dear Department Chair" or "Dear Provost" and include three parts: 1) a reflection on the author's own career trajectory; 2) ideas about the addressee's particular duties and lessons learned in the role; and 3) recommendations for success and efficacy. Letters also give directives to current administrators and those in charge of next-generation leadership development.

The conversation around the Netflix comedy series *The Chair*, starring Golden Globe Award–winning actor Sandra Oh, demonstrated there is enduring popular interest in higher education administration. Unfortunately, the show spotlights the woman of color department chair's sexuality more than her leadership, she is removed from her chair position in the first year of holding the job, and the show was cancelled after one season. This is a sadly accurate representation of how women of color in the chair position are often misrepresented, disrespected, and not given due consideration—and are often held responsible for cleaning up the mess left by others or who must take the fall for events not fully in their control. This volume seeks to specifically address the next generation of academic leaders by unpacking the roles of chair, dean, provost, president, and all related leadership team positions. These readings are especially geared toward faculty and women of color who aspire to leadership positions but who are underinformed, discouraged, or intimidated by the idea of pursuing a lead role.

As a preface to the chapters in this collection, each of the three editors offers letters of insight and encouragement below. We hope you find, as we have, places to connect, celebrate, reflect, and grow your network that will give new meaning to higher education leadership and service.

Stephanie Evans: What Do Department Chairs Do? Everything. But You Can Do It . . . Well.

When I entered higher education as a first-generation, low-income, adult re-entry student, I had very little conception of the role of department chair. As an undergraduate, I knew that the chair was the complaint department if anything went wrong on campus or in the classroom. When I entered graduate school, I knew the chair (along with the graduate advisor) was a key point of contact for my welcome, acculturation, and training in the profession. When I entered the professoriate, the department chair (along with the hiring committee and faculty mentor) was central to my onboarding. As a newly tenured faculty elected to the post in 2010, I knew that a vote of confidence by faculty to lead the unit was a serious responsibility. At no point did I truly understand that the role of chair is the central hub in the wheel of the university.

I learned from my advisor, John H. Bracey, Jr., that one should approach being chair as an act of service to the unit, the people, and the campus—that it is NOT to be used as a ladder rung for personal privilege, to impress people and demand fealty, or to punish others. When I was appointed to the position, I learned quickly that the chair is a gateway post for upper administration. Chair is a position of never-ending pressure because it is the only forward-facing position that has accountability to *every* corner of the campus.

As outlined in the concluding section of this chapter, the chair's job involves facilitating numerous moving parts: the creation and implementation of a department vision, daily operations, budget, promotions, hiring and firing, scholarship, research support for students and faculty, class scheduling, teaching, mentorship, mediation, and more and more and more. Although this book is written for all administrators, the focus is on the department chair because it is the role with the most responsibility—and if chairs have no support, deans, provosts, and presidents also can't be fully successful. Sustainable leadership in higher education depends on support for chairs.

I have held unit leadership positions at three very different institutions: a large, predominantly white (PWI), Research I, flagship institution in a small southern town; a private, teaching-focused, research-intensive Historically Black College and University (HBCU) in a large southern city; and a large, majority-minority, rapidly growing R1 in a big southern city. My experience as chair in three departments over the past twelve years has yielded many realizations along the lines of those raised by authors in this volume.

In answer to the question "What Do Department Chairs Do?" I published an extensive job description in the July 2021 journal *The Department Chair*. This detailed list of the numerous tasks, skills, and areas of accountability involved in this pivotal administrative position is provided as a closing section of this chapter in order to fully expose the breadth and depth of the role.

Race and gender are dynamic variables that can often make an already hard job more difficult. Though the position is certainly arduous at times, there are ways to manage the task of "everything" one must do and to do the work in a way that sustains the spirit as well as the profession. Focusing on wellness and balance as a daily practice can help manage what is imperative and what is not. Knowing the job is half the battle. Learning how to prioritize the "big rocks" and doing first things first is another significant part.

I would not have made it through the twelve years as department chair without a network of Black women academics who could empathize with me about the huge stressors the job holds. Regardless of a person's individual experience as an academic administrator, this collection helps normalize the idea of Black women unit heads by centering those who have held the position. Black women's experiences offer higher education a unique locale from which to define work-life balance and chart a course for institutional change. Too often, the academy normalizes chronic stress instead of fostering a culture of wellness at work. A healthy chair cohort can make a difference in academe by establishing practices that create cultures of collective progress, but without conscious support for faculty leaders, burnout is probable, as those in leadership positions during the 2020 public health, political, and racial upheavals can affirm. Administration must move beyond "wellness days" and begin to create and sustain policy decisions (like protecting academic freedom and employing proper staff support) that lessen the need for mental health breaks.

Tenure-track research, teaching, and moves toward deanship or upper administration are sometimes on the radar of burgeoning academics, but becoming department chair seems to happen to outstanding faculty who are caught unawares or who take the position only with reservations. This collection of voices can enable more formal discussions among junior faculty as well as senior colleagues about the value and professional benefit of gaining department head leadership experience, as well as what constitutes desirable character traits for the position. This increased awareness of the actual role of department chair can go a long way toward demystifying unit politics and processes for incoming faculty. This information can also fuel more purposeful selection of unit leaders from senior faculty, and perhaps a more purposeful cultivation of leadership from underrepresented populations in particular fields. As the student population diversifies, so should the faculty, unit leadership, and upper administration. In 2021, after the Nikole Hannah-Jones debacle, the *Chronicle of Higher Education* rightly acknowledged the lack of diversity in university boards of trustees. This collection includes the perspective of one of the few University Regents or Board Chairs in the country—in addition to the first Black woman to lead a university press—bringing together viewpoints from all levels of leadership to promote more informed collaboration. These voices should be joined by legions of diverse leaders in the near future because single representation is tokenism and not enough to facilitate fundamental change.

For those taking on the role of chair, associate chair, dean, associate dean, vice president, or provost, the road is especially rough, since you are accountable but not always the final decision maker. Below, I offer recommendations grounded in Rosalyn Terborg-Penn's foundational articulation of African Feminist Values: self-care and collective care. Following those tips, I include a list of five characteristics of what I call #HistoricalWellness and mental health practices that I've used over the years to get me through the most challenging days.

In the introduction to the edited volume *Women in Africa and the African Diaspora* (1996), Dr. Terborg-Penn writes,

> Perhaps the two most dominant values in the African feminist theory, which can be traced through a time perspective into the New World, are developing survival strategies and encouraging self-reliance through female networks.

The imperative to teach humane values, pay attention to individual needs, and work collaboratively with others resonates in the work of writers like Toni Morrison, Bernice Johnson Reagon, and Angela Davis, each of whom embodies the National Association of Colored Women's motto, "lifting as we climb." Essentially, the recommendations below reflect a need to balance compassion for one's self and compassion for others in the academic unit, in the campus community, and in the world. There are many gems offered in the *Palimpsest* journal, *The Department Chair* journal, and in this current collection that unpack the tasks of academic administrative jobs and give useful tips. To those helpful hints, I would add the following:

Self-Care (Survival)

- **Prioritize self-care and self-compassion.** Try a little tenderness. Be kind to yourself. You will not be perfect. Don't expect perfection from yourself and you won't be disappointed. Self-compassion is the cornerstone of compassion for others.
- **Manage your time and energy.** Manage your calendar closely—even if you have an assistant. Require all action requests in writing. Create a culture of written contact to ease workflow and efficacy—you will never remember the myriad requests and keep them in order without having them written down. Written documentation might help you keep track of the nature and status of all requests, as well as your responses to them and follow-up steps. That said, don't hammer people with emails all day, every day. Don't use email as a weapon.

  Develop a system for quickly filing, deleting, or answering emails—if you don't manage your system of information intake, every day will be a losing fight against the quicksand inbox. Have some open office hours but rely mainly on appointments, so colleagues and other community members can count on you being available for drop-ins, but also know they can have a time dedicated to them for a specific request. Make use of more than one office on campus. Find a library space or lab space where you can work without interruption. Don't stay there all the time. Use the space for a *focus day*—a day or a series of half days during the week when you can answer emails, work on that report, follow up with colleagues about requests, start or finish a big-picture task, or complete other work that requires your full attention, while still being on campus for emergency issues. Self-care is essential and time management is central to self-care. No one will give you a break . . . you must take one when you need one.

- **Read the handbooks, know the full job description, and calibrate your role toward best practices in the profession.** Download or bookmark all faculty, student, department, college, and university manuals. Become familiar with standards in your field at similar institutions so you have context for your institution. Look up chair books, guides, and resources to help you deal with issues that arise with students, faculty, administrators, and other areas of campus. Before reaching out to ask a question about how to handle something, read the handbook. If an issue grows into a documented problem, the first thing a student, colleague, parent, dean, or legal counsel might ask will reference policy. Start there—even if you deviate from the policy, you will have a rationale about why you made a decision. Then call others to verify that your reading of the policy is in line with university culture. Be careful of "off the record" conversations. If folks won't put something in writing, sometimes it may mean they won't stand by comments and you will be left holding the bag. Sometimes, however, offline conversations can clear things up in a way writing cannot. Learn to discern.

  Read the university strategic plan so you can create your departmental plan with context. Balance all policies and practices with professional and humane ethics—identify areas where the handbook must be revised to reflect a more fair or just practice. Learn your job in context of a network of national and professional standards. Don't fall into the lull of "this is MY leadership style," or "this is how we do it here." Learn from your peers nationally and be open to learning from others who have other life and work experiences. As Colette Taylor and Johnnetta Cole both state, lead with humility—you won't always be right. Move the system toward justice and make humane practice the "best practice."

- **Document your work.** Make sure to keep records of
  your challenges, accomplishments, and actions. News-
  letters are a convenient way to chronicle your contributions in shaping a department. Reflect after every
  semester and every year to chronicle steps you took,
  practices you institutionalized, services you provided,
  and lessons you learned. Measure your personal, professional, and institutional growth. Don't wait until it is all
  over to look back, look inward, or look forward. Mark
  progress and pay attention in real time and keep a professional archive so your accomplishments don't get lost
  or appropriated by others. Maintain a record of all emails
  and written communication . . . even after you have left
  a post. Receipts, receipts, receipts.
- **Keep researching what you love.** My work on mental
  health, self-care, and inner peace developed out of a
  work-life balance crisis. Now that I have incorporated
  those topics into my research agenda, they have also
  manifested in other areas of my work. Do not wait for
  large chunks of time to write; build it into your daily and
  weekly routines and task lists. Maya Angelou's poem
  "Still I Rise" might serve as an inspiration. Write to
  RISE: write to Remember your intellectual foremothers, to Immerse yourself in the present moment, to Study
  the academic process, and to Enjoy writing in ways that
  build community.

Collective Care (Self-Reliance in Network)
- **Do not be a boss.** Boss mentality is oppressive and pred-
  atory. Respect and support work and workers—including
  unions. Be kind to others—they don't owe you or
  the institution their life. *Do not be a boss.* Folks will
  have different work ethics, habits, motivations, and
  experiences—focus on the task at hand, not on trying
  to control other human beings. Toni Morrison said,
  "If you can only be tall because somebody is on their
  knees, then you have a serious problem." *Do not be a boss.*

You will have co-workers and those whom you supervise. Yes, you will have to let some people go and free them of their job, but don't let go of your humanity and free yourself of credibility in the process. You are not an overseer—slavery is not the goal and the university should not be run like a plantation. Do your job as well as you can and expect the same of others. Offer support—with power comes responsibility. Don't traumatize people by reminding them you're "the boss." *Do not be a boss.* While Black women often get a bad rap for being aggressive, sometimes we are the aggressor, including to other minoritized faculty, staff, or students in our units. *Do not be a boss.* Better to be a coach with a team than a boss with oppressed workers. You will have to fall on some swords, lose some arguments, be magnanimous to those who don't deserve it, and swallow some pride. Do it. Don't be a horse's ass—don't be a boss. If you are put in a position where the mandate is to oppress others, fight back and, if necessary, walk away.

- **Organize.** Create formal and informal networks of department chairs within and beyond your campus. Take advantage of institution-wide group meetings but also create spaces where you can share information with an appreciation for some confidentiality. Upper administration may see chair organization as a threat to established order and protocols, but it is actually a vital opportunity to centrally stabilize and improve the institution and solve problems at a system level. Chairs need a lifeline with folks who can empathize and strategize. Upper administration might encourage informal spaces and create formal spaces for chairs to organize—it could make everyone's work more effective and address problems across campus.

- **Appreciate your network, but don't rely on nepotism and cliques.** I have learned of several instances where those not in the "in" group were targeted or not supported because they did not have enough social capital. Expand your network to include those who don't have access to the most resources and to those with whom you don't always agree. If you can't be supportive, leave folks alone.

- **Don't seek to be the only one or the main one.** You are special, but not that special. I'm a professional with a solid track record for being an outstanding academic. So are the other three Black women named Stephanie who are associated with this project. There is more than enough room in higher education for excellent Black women academics. Find them, support them, and let them support you. As President Cole said in her Foreword, cultivate a collaborative leadership style that engages and creates space for other marginalized people. This especially includes queer and transgender people and other women of color, people with disabilities, divergent learners, and everybody else on the margins.

- **Tell the truth.** Above all, be ethical, equitable, and act in good faith. Your reputation for fairness (or unfairness) will come back to you in due time. Be consistent and develop a rationale that you stick to for all decision making. Create a culture of transparency. Note how many people around you do not tell the truth; do not forget if they lie about others, they are going to lie about you too. You will be lied about, 'buked, cheated, and scorned; expect it and don't retaliate by replicating those bad practices. I have been lied about in some very hurtful ways by people who don't know I'm aware of their lies. They were blatant lies so I did not grace them with my attention. Yet, I have never forgotten how it made me feel. So I don't do that to others. I have also been maligned by people who smile in my face. I've removed myself from their presence so they no longer have the opportunity to do so. Someone once called me "nicety"—nice nasty. It's true that I don't often deign to argue with people. But I'm not a liar. Don't lie—there is no need.

- **Assess before you act.** Survey all parties when you enter the position (undergraduate and graduate students, faculty, administrators, alumni, community partners, former chairs, and campus partners). Use a basic SWOT analysis: strengths, weaknesses, opportunities, threats—and then modify this to your needs. (Donna Nicol brilliantly names this "getting all the tea.") Surveys will give those who may not make it to events an opportunity to give you insights, as well as provide you with a baseline of experiences, perceptions, and expectations. Keep the survey short (ten questions or fewer) and include open-ended answers so respondents have a chance to elaborate. Ask people open-ended questions like: Who are you? What do you want? What would you like to contribute? You may be surprised at the answers.

In addition to a written survey, create opportunities for face-to-face discussion. Don't make the listening tour perfunctory; act on information others offer. Don't be a dictator. If you seek to get rid of everyone you don't like, who doesn't like you, or with whom you disagree, you will be surrounded by sycophants. Learn to work with people you don't like and create opportunities for all to thrive, despite differences of opinion or approaches. It's called being an adult. Understand that relationships are dynamic and complex. Your bestie might be someone else's worst enemy. Above all, be professional and ethical with everyone—friend or not.

- **Have a network of mentors and build a community of colleagues for peer mentoring.** I have relied on many mentors over the years. Make sure you seek out numerous people for advice; don't rely on only one or two people. Whether or not you have a formal chair orientation, locate formal and informal mentors who can help you navigate the tasks and politics you will face. Several books are also available to help you better understand the position of chair or director; these books will help you anticipate some problems that may arise and see them as normal and manageable, rather than as particular and alarming.

- **Build a succession plan into your department plan.**
  Whether you plan to stay in the role of chair for a limited
  time (usually three years) or are invited to remain for a
  longer period, normalize leadership training and prepare
  everyone for your inevitable departure. While some chairs
  and administrators serve for a dozen years or more, most
  don't. Regardless of when your time comes to move out
  of the position of chair, prepare yourself and those around
  you (administration, peers, and students) for a smooth
  transition by paving the way for the next unit leader. In
  my most recent position, after the departure of the other
  two Black women faculty from our department, I stepped
  down a semester early and facilitated a smooth transition to my successor because we had already established
  working relationships. The dean was not excited about my
  decision to step down early, but her selection was a known
  factor to the department, so it truly was a win-win. I was
  immediately able to take up some of the service tasks of
  the departed faculty, and the new chair was able to come
  in and lead the unit knowing she had my full support.
  Build relationships and plan ahead. Do what is best for
  you, even if others are not thrilled about it.
- **Prioritize wellness—for yourself AND others.**
  Research about self-care and balance has increased significantly in the years between the 2016 presidential election and the 2021 pandemic and racial uprisings in the
  United States. That does not mean folks have improved
  in care for self and others—only that there is a general
  awareness of how we are collectively operating under
  duress. Prioritize wellness for yourself—daily—and you
  will at once model how to do so and be better prepared to
  work with the tasks and demands of sitting in the chair
  or another administrative role. Sit in the chair—but don't
  let the chair kill you. If you need to step away from the
  position for health or principle, do so without hesitation,
  but do facilitate the transfer as much as possible—your
  decision will deeply impact many others as well. Also,

if you demand the right to say no, you have to create space for others to do so as well—without recrimination. Everyone does not have to agree with you or like what you do. There will not be total consensus about your performance—and that is ok. Do what you can and leave the rest alone.

Department chair leadership comes with a unique set of challenges and rewards that speak to the particular geographic or institutional environment where one works, but there is also significant overlap—as this collection reveals—regardless of the location in which we work.

Institutionalize Wellness: Six Mental Health Practices (MENTAL)

In addition to the values of self-care and collective care above, I suggest embracing chair work as a practice of mental health and wellness. Influenced by the stress research in Robert Sapolsky's *Why Zebras Don't Have Ulcers*, I characterize historical wellness and my own practice with an acronym, MENTAL, representing the six most effective stress management strategies. These six practices are as follows:

MEDITATE—sit still. Take at least five minutes each morning and each evening to breathe. Don't reflect, think, or plan . . . just breathe.

EXERCISE—move. Sitting in the chair for twelve years made my body stiff. That is one of the reasons I incorporated the study of yoga into my research. Do what you love to keep your body moving and release the pressure in your head.

NETWORK—ask for and provide social support. Even as an experienced chair, I found myself sinking. Reaching out to others to create the Chair at the Table network empowered me to move forward in solidarity and joy. Keep your social support system of family, friends, and *framily* (especially academic sisters) close—you need them and they need you.

TRUST—have faith. If you are a praying person, pray. However you express spirituality, embrace it as central to developing and maintaining your whole being.

ADVOCATE—ask for what you want and push for what you need. One of the main responsibilities of leadership is to advocate for resources and to amplify those whose voices are not generally heard by leaders at higher levels. You may not be able to control outcomes and decisions around campus, but you can at least identify the changes that can be made where possible.

LEARN—study your job. Study higher education. Study the world. Nourish your brain and feed your soul. Academe can be a soul-sucking place—find a library, a tea garden, a skating rink, or some other creative space in your life where you take time to continuously prune, cultivate, and grow your SELF.

In closing,

Higher education administration is extremely difficult. After myriad other difficulties getting to this point (chronicled in several books by women of color students and faculty), I wish I could share some news about rest and ease. Alas, that is not the case.

Given historical expectations of constant caretaking and limitless service by Black women, a mantle of martyrdom thrust on Black faculty, and racist-sexist stereotypes about leadership, the role of chair presents inevitable challenges for Black women. This leadership role constitutes a unique administrative assignment, as cultural identity within a department impacts power dynamics, peer relationships, conflict resolution, and communication with various campus communities. Middle management always puts academicians in the squeeze, but the position of chair as a central hub of activity also positions Black women to voice our experiences in ways that can fundamentally improve higher education at a root level, positively impacting the entire university. One of the takeaway messages from this collection is the need for upper administration to focus on expanding support for department chairs—and discussions like these can equip deans, associate deans, provosts, vice presidents, presidents, and boards to do so.

The groundbreaking book *Telling Histories: Black Women Historians in the Ivory Tower* paid homage to Anna Julia Cooper and Marion Thompson Wright as foremothers in the field of history. Here, I recognize Anna Julia Cooper and Mary McLeod Bethune as academic administrators in whose footsteps we follow. Both, in their own ways, radiated leadership at their institutions, which connected them and their students to scholars around the globe. Though we are just getting to a critical mass of administrative leaders, there are several generations of Black women in higher education who have paved the way to leadership, including Cooper, Bethune, and Willa Player. Player was president of Bennett College from 1956 to 1966; I wrote about her and others in *Black Women in the Ivory Tower, 1850–1954: An Intellectual History* (2007). Dr. Player modeled what she called a leadership of inclusiveness, characterized by love, sanity, and a balance between science and moral responsibility.

Authors in this current volume embody these historical values and show how they operate in the twenty-first-century academy. You are not the first to do this work—be purposeful in identifying those who came before you for inspiration and instruction. You can do good work, you can do hard work well . . . and, yes, you can be well in the process.

—*Dr. Evans*

Stephanie Shonekan: "Unbow Your Head, Sister!"

Dear Dean,

"Unbow your head, sister"—This is one of my all-time favorite movie lines. In Barry Jenkins's *If Beale Street Could Talk* (2018), based on the James Baldwin book of the same title, the older sister says it to the younger sister when the latter is feeling down and disappointed in herself. That line stopped me in my tracks because it reminded me of all the ways that I have experienced sisterhood as the big sister—encouraging other women in the profession—and as the little sister—when I have needed to hear encouragement and affirmation from others. That line is clear in its direction—stop feeling that you are unworthy, shake it off, chin up, walk forward to your destiny. But in that tender moment between sisters, there's also a silent acknowledgment that the odds are stacked against us. And yet we must move forward. The line conjures images of generations of stoic Black women who have been bearers of the tradition, preservers of the culture, keepers of the village in a world that does not see us. It communicates an unequivocal urgency to refuse erasure and oppression. And, most importantly, it signifies a tight bond, a sisterhood that is dependable and unshakable. I do not know what I would have done on my journey into administration and through life without hearing this direction from a number of sisters, from mentors, from peers and mentees.

I see this book as an elaboration of that line. Each chapter is another way of saying "Unbow your head, sister!" The impetus for this project was ignited by a string of experiences. In 2022, I asked my co-editors, Stephanie Evans and Stephanie Adams, to do some workshops for junior URM faculty and senior administrators at the University of Missouri, where I was at the time. I knew that their expertise and experience could help these groups to do some collective soul-searching about how to improve our culture of mentorship and menteeship here. And they did not hesitate to say yes because we had already built up a sisterhood. When they visited Mizzou, as I moderated the sessions and presented their wisdom to our faculty/ administrator groups, our natural camaraderie was noticed and a number of people suggested lightheartedly that we should "take the show on the road!" So, the Stephanies (as we fondly call ourselves) reached out to other sisters we knew who had experience worth sharing in this book.

Whom do we hope to share this with? Of course, with our other sisters who are considering or are already on the path to university administration. We want to encourage them, offer our own experiences, and tell them to unbow their heads. But also, we want to share this with others—with the kinds of audiences that the Stephanies encountered at Mizzou—faculty of color and administrators who need to be enlightened and brought along in understanding what all faculty need to succeed. So, while this book is primarily for our sisters, it is also for others who need to come to terms with the incredible challenges we face in the academy as women of color. These challenges are ever-present in our everyday encounters. For example, I recently attended a leadership training where consultants were offering some data on student satisfaction with higher education. There were three bullet points on a PowerPoint slide: one showed the overall percentage of satisfaction among all students surveyed; next was the percentage for students of color; and the third was the percentage for women. As the audience gasped at the dropping percentages, I waited in vain for the fourth point, because Black women were not fully represented in this data. Finally I put my hand up and asked: "What about the people who stand at the intersection of race and gender, i.e., Black women?"

The consultant—a white woman—looked shocked and said that was something they had not thought to disaggregate from the data set. This episode reminded me how little we are thought of by the mainstream. They think generally of people of color, and of women, but they do not attend closely to women of color. I hope folks beyond the sisterhood pick this book up as a valuable source for getting the information they need to support women who are not white at their institutions.

But this book is primarily for our sisters. The importance of sisterhood on this journey cannot be overemphasized. As an ethnomusicologist who studies Black music, I think of certain tracks that form the soundtrack for our journey. I'd like to cite two songs here. "Count on Me" by Whitney Houston and Cece Winans is the last song on the *Waiting to Exhale* soundtrack by Babyface (1995). Whitney and Cece deliver a beautiful message that is underlined by the fact that they had a beautiful, sustaining friendship in real life. Every time I hear that song, it reminds me of how we rely on each other as Black women. I became chair of the Department of Black Studies at Mizzou at a time when I was not sure I was ready for the challenge. It was senior Black women faculty like April Langley (included in this volume), Flore Zephir, Tola Pearce, and Lisa Brock (my chair/mentor from my previous job at Columbia College Chicago) who encouraged me to rise to the occasion. I was ready, they told me, to take the reins of leadership, and I knew I could lean on them whenever

I needed to get advice. I was the only Black chair in the college and could have found myself isolated, but these women reminded me to "unbow my head." In that first year of my tenure as chair of the Department of Black Studies at Mizzou, our students protested and I was launched into the spotlight because the community and news media had no way of processing what was happening, so they approached me. Knowing I had a sisterhood behind me, I lifted my head and spoke about what the students were going through, about how the history of our field was built on movements like this, and I encouraged other faculty and administrators to support the move for positive change on our campus.

Another episode I think about when I hear the song "Count on Me" occurred in 2018, when I accepted the position of chair of the W. E. B. Du Bois Department of Afro-American Studies at the University of Massachusetts, a historical department that had produced a number of stellar scholars. A new chair from outside the institution is always received with some hesitation by the students, faculty, former chairs, and alumni. Along with a wonderful administrative manager, Trish Loveland, three other important women helped me settle into that position. Dr. Esther Terry, the only other Black woman who had ever led the department; Dr. Joye Bowman, associate dean of the College of Humanities and Fine Art; and Dr. Stephanie Evans, arguably the most decorated alumna from the program (and co-editor of this book). Each of these women answered my call whenever I needed a lift. I could not have succeeded in that position without each of them and their support.

Sisters, you will know when it is time to move to the next rung of this academic leadership ladder. Each of us, as co-editors, has considered that moment when we might be approached by a search firm or a senior colleague to consider the next level of leadership. The truth is, we already have what we need to proceed. In addition to an awareness of the organizational and work-life balance skills you will read about throughout this book, by the time you serve as chair you have already built a strong network of support you can count on. I could have remained chair for years, but knew I was ready to move into a deanship because I had the skill set and the support. I knew that, as Whitney and Cece sing in "Count on Me," I could reach out to my mentors "through thick and thin." As I began my position as Dean at the University of Maryland, a new group of Black women emerged, expanding my network and reinforcing the stability of the ground I would be standing on. This network also includes some empathetic non-Black folks, but it is people of color who understand my unique journey and the challenges I encounter as a Black woman. I guard my ground carefully as I continue to learn and grow in my position.

The second musical example I would like to cite is the collaboration between Nina Simone and Miriam Makeba on a song called "Thulasizwe," which was featured on a 1991 album by Makeba. This musical sisterhood of two iconic Black women reminds me of what is possible in the building of bridges between African women and women of African descent throughout the Diaspora. Too often, we see a chasm in the relationships between folks in Africa and the Diaspora. Our histories, at the same time distinct and deeply connected, have resulted in miseducation, suspicion, and division. But if we can approach our common ground, we can be formidable. As someone who was raised in Nigeria by a Trinidadian mother, I knew I had a lot to learn when I ventured into African American Studies so long ago. Over the years I have worked on that bridge, building it brick by brick, learning about my sisters from other parts of the Black world. The song by Makeba and Simone depicts the power in their relationship. Both had endured so much as Black women—in South Africa and in the United States. There was a shared experience that they recognized in each other. And when it was time to celebrate Nelson Mandela, in typical Black woman style, they came together to lift up the brother in "Thulasizwe."

In the song, Makeba and Simone repeat the line "I shall be released." Though it's referring to Mandela's journey to freedom, this line could not be a better depiction of what we do for each other as Black women. We release each other from the bonds of oppression and erasure that white supremacy has designed for us. We refuse to be restrained by our collective and personal histories.

I am so proud that this book includes women of so many different identities in the Black world, from small towns to large cities in the United States, and from the Caribbean and Africa. Like Makeba and Simone, we move forward together, despite the incredible odds that have been mounted against us. So much of what sustains us as professional Black women are our families. Indeed, I am blessed with a wonderful spouse, children, and siblings, who love and support me. But I also cannot say enough about the importance of sisterhood that we build within and beyond the boundaries of the work environment. When we need to breathe and refresh, we can rest in those friendships with other women who understand what it means to be Black in the academy. I have close "sista-scholars" who I run to when I need to vent, cry, and celebrate. We write together, laugh raucously together, contend with life together, and remind ourselves to unbow our heads every step of the way.

—*Dr. Shonekan*

Stephanie Adams: Just Run Your Own Race

Dear Future Dean,

Some time ago I read the book *The Right Words at the Right Time* by Marlo Thomas and Friends. Marlo, a well-known actress in her own right, is the daughter of Danny Thomas, famous actor and founder of St. Jude Children's Research Hospital. In the book she shares that her dad encouraged her to "just run your own race" when she told him she wanted to change her last name as she decided to follow his footsteps into the acting profession. These words have guided me throughout my career and reinforced my desire to follow my own path, which some would describe as non-traditional, but it has served me well these past twenty-three years. I hope this counsel, along with the following lessons, serve you well as you embark on your own journey through the academy.

PURSUE YOUR PASSION

From the time I was seven I wanted to be a physician, but in ninth grade I injured my knee for the first time and decided I would become a biomedical engineer and orthopedic surgeon. Every decision I made was with this goal in mind. Then one day after a series of gut-wrenching experiences, I decided this was not the path for me and a change must be made. I did quite a bit of soul-searching to figure out what really excited me. Having spent most of my formative years on college campuses, as my dad was an academic leader, I realized I was passionate about working with students and wanted to create programs to facilitate success for engineering students. Thus, I set my sights on becoming the associate dean of academic affairs at a college of engineering. This goal led me to pursue my PhD and a career in the academy. It also carried me through the trials and tribulations of my doctoral studies, the joys and challenges of teaching, conducting research and pursuing tenure. It also prompted me to pursue my first administrative position at a point in my career when nearly everyone counseled against it. I believe that these people had good intentions and wanted me to be successful, but I had to explore what I thought would make me happy and I think it has worked well for me. Pursuing my passion—working with and creating programs for students—made it easier to put in the time and work necessary to be successful, while providing me unwavering motivation to achieve. In the words of Confucius, "If you choose a job you love, you'll never have to work a day in your life." So do what you love.

CHOOSE WISELY: ENVIRONMENT MATTERS

It is important to find an environment that will help you thrive, not just survive, in the early part of your career. In my case that was the University of Nebraska, Lincoln. I had only been to Nebraska once before my interview, and that was in the back seat of my parents' Volkswagen camper van. But I ended up in a place that needed what I had to offer. A place that allowed me to pursue my personal teaching and research goals. A place that valued my contributions while supporting my growth and development as a faculty member. I found that I could be myself and pursue work that I was passionate about. This doesn't mean it was always easy, but it was where I found success. For more about this experience, I direct you to my chapter entitled "Succeeding in the Face of Doubt" in Christine Stanley's 2006 book, *Faculty of Color: Teaching in Predominantly White Colleges and Universities*.

FORM AND LEVERAGE A MENTOR NETWORK

For as long as I can remember I've always sought the counsel of those I found to be wise, who were living a life I thought I wanted or had been where I wanted go. It has been crucial to my career success that members of this ever-growing network were willing to share their experiences and career advice with me. The individuals who were part of this network emerged from a variety of associations: faculty and administrators from undergrad, my graduate advisors, people hired at the same time as I was, people from my college but in other departments, people on campus but from other colleges, people outside of my institutions but within the field, and people from non-related disciplines who've inspired me. The mentors who have had the greatest impact on my career are those who sought to really understand me as an individual and the institutional environment I was in, who encouraged me to pursue work that was exciting and meaningful to me, and to forge a path where I would be productive and happy. My mentors also helped me navigate my imposter syndrome feelings by filling in the holes in my confidence, until my own confidence kicked in.

I encourage you to seek mentors at each juncture of your career: people who will provide personal support when things get tough and who will advocate for you when you least expect it. In 2004 I decided I wanted to be a university president, and I shared this goal with several of my mentors. The next thing I knew, I received an invitation to an American Council on Education: Women of Color conference. This invitation-only event was life-changing and empowering. To this day, I still have no idea who gave them my name, but I am so glad someone did. The support of mentors is immeasurable.

MAINTAIN WORK-LIFE BALANCE

Though I have not done such a great job at this, I recognize how important it is to find your own balance between your personal life and work. We all need to seek and engage in our passions outside of work. Find things that bring you joy, calm you, inspire you, and provide you with breaks from the grind of the academy. For me it has been my love of music, travel, learning from others, golf, and photography. I have relied on each of these pursuits to sustain and motivate me throughout my career. They have been a source of strength during trying times and challenges. They have allowed me to escape, regroup, and re-emerge stronger. I only wish I had done a better job of taking care of my physical vessel. A sports injury at sixteen has literally slowed and weighed me down for decades. Only recently have I fully prioritized my own well-being. As the flight attendants say in the safety briefing, "place your own mask on first and then assist others." I wish I had done more caring for myself rather than for others. Not to be selfish, but it makes a huge difference.

Lastly, I want to encourage you to keep learning and to have fun. On many occasions you will not have all the answers or be the smartest one in the room; lifelong learning will help you to find success, personally and professionally. I learn something new almost daily. But even more important than book learning, or learning from others, is learning from yourself. Spend time reflecting and getting to know yourself: what you value, what makes you tick, what ticks you off, etc. Then embrace strategies to mitigate these shortcomings that you will undoubtedly experience.

Former football coach Bum Phillips is credited with saying this: "Winning is only half of it. Having fun is the other half." While I have been successful by most accounts, the most important thing for me has been enjoying the journey. This journey has taken me to over fifty countries and provided an opportunity to see some of the greatest treasures of the world. The journey wasn't always linear and it presented challenges and self-doubt, but my internal desire to pursue excellence has been fulfilling and satisfying. It has led to a quality of life many have only experienced in their dreams, and to very few, if any, regrets. So, Dean Stephanie Adams, as Danny Thomas told Marlo, "I raised you to be a thoroughbred. When thoroughbreds run, they wear blinders to keep their eyes focused straight ahead with no distractions . . . You Just Run Your Own Race."

—*Dr. Adams*

Conclusion: Thank You for the Very Difficult Job You Have Chosen to Do

Again, THANK YOU for sitting in the chair; for leading beyond the table; and for sharing your time, energy, and talent for the benefit of others. Each author in this book reflects on experiential challenges, celebrations, and lessons, and offers recommendations in the form of pro tips, insights, feedback, and suggestions for change. Our discussion builds on existing primers and toolkits by expanding the reading audience to include all campus partners, particularly those who work with diversity initiatives.

The majority of authors in this volume focus on experiences that foreground race and gender studies, which provide nuanced analysis regarding the responsibilities of unit leadership in marginalized academic areas. As mentioned earlier in this chapter, in line with nationwide commemorative events, the Department of African American and Diaspora Studies and the Callie House Center at Vanderbilt University hosted a fall 2019 symposium. This gathering advanced dialogue around the first fifty years of mainstream, institutionalized critical race and gender research. The clear intent of the symposium was to draw attention to the role of chair in order to attract more Black women to this important role. At the online workshop held as a follow-up in January 2021, presenters offered a series of panel presentations. Over a hundred registrants indicated significant interest in the next generation of department chairs, deans, provosts, and beyond.

Below is a reprint of "The Department Chair Job Description," initially published in the Summer 2021 issue of *The Department Chair*, which codifies and categorizes the numerous disparate tasks required of the chair and the skills necessary for the job. The expansiveness of this description and recurring themes from initial Chair at the Table events demonstrates that this book should be part of a growing conversation about the many dimensions of chair and administrative work.

Sincerely,
The Stephanies

Department Chair Job Description, Stephanie Y. Evans, 2021

Tasks (Accountability)
1. Academic Unit Head
    a. Leadership & Management (see *Skills*)
2. Research
    a. Conception, Proposal, & Grants
    b. Reading, Investigation, & Writing
    c. Submission & Revision
    d. Dissemination & Application
3. Teaching
    a. Syllabus Construction & Preparation
    b. Instruction & Grading
    c. Student Development
4. Service
    a. Campus Committees
    b. Letters of Recommendation
    c. Manuscript, T & P Peer Review
    d. Professional Organizations
5. Upper Administration Liaison
    a. Dean, Provost, President, & Board
6. Department Admin
    a. Budget, Fiscal, Facilities, & Equipment
    b. Staff & Student Staff
    c. Faculty (Recruit, Hire, Onboard, Evaluate, Retain, Tenure and Promote, Furlough, & Release)
    d. Students (Recruit, Advise, Supervise, Support, Mentor, Manage Requests)
    e. Curriculum, Scheduling, Enrollment, & Assessment
    f. Bylaws, Catalogs, & Accreditation
    g. Records & Reports
    h. Meetings & Newsletters
    i. Department Committees, Executive Committee, & Advisory Board
7. Campus Community
    a. Disciplinary Expertise (Scholarly Panels & Services), Chair's Councils, Faculty Senate, Foundation Sponsors

      and Development, Fellowships, Feeder Programs, & Consortia
- b. Admissions, Academic Affairs, Registrar
- c. Student Affairs & Counseling Centers
- d. Parents, Family of Students, & Alumni
- e. Institutional Review & Reporting, Accrediting Agencies, Service Learning, Extension Offices, & Unions
8. Local, National, & International Communities
9. Other Duties as Assigned or Required

Skills (Responsibility)
1. Leadership
   a. Leadership Values & Leadership Philosophy
   b. Decision Making that is
      i. Ethical
      ii. Equitable
      iii. Consistent
      iv. Transparent
   c. Interpersonal Relations: Effective Oral & Written Communication, Problem Solving Strategies
   d. Advocate for the Unit; Maintain Department Identity, Environment, Culture, Representation, Image, & Morale
   e. Create Collegial Environment & Coordinate Cross-Campus Collaboration
   f. Maintain Excellence, Enhance Standing in the Discipline, Provide Disciplinary Innovations
   g. Diversity, Equity & Inclusion (DEI) / Social Justice
   h. Mentoring, Support, Professional Development, Leadership Development, & Succession Planning
2. Management
   a. Interpret, Create, & Implement Policy
   b. Create/Maintain Unit Mission, Vision, Goals, & Strategic Plan in line with University Mission
   c. Define/Support Institutional Goals, Ensure Legality, & Maintain Safety
   d. Administrative Information
      i. Locate & Analyze Data

    ii. Independent Judgment

    iii. Media Management

  e. Time Management

    i. Work-Life Balance

    ii. To-Do Lists, Meetings, & Emails

  f. Stress Management

    i. Boundaries

    ii. Mental and Holistic Health

  g. Climate, Complaint, & Conflict Management

  h. Crisis Management

  i. Unit Health & Trauma Management

    i. Harm Reduction & Restorative Justice

  j. Issues, Trends, and Events

    i. Technology & Online Teaching

    ii. Elections & State/National/Global Politics

    iii. Era-defining Events (e.g., COVID-19 Pandemic, 2021 Political Crisis, or ongoing Environmental Disasters)

In the article that accompanies the job description, "Meditations from a Black Woman Chair: Social Justice Values and a New Normal in Academic Administration," Evans writes about the challenges facing unit heads. The public health crisis that hit in 2020 created impossible circumstances, with department chairs "charged with managing stress during a global pandemic that has, thus far, killed three million people, including more than five hundred thousand in the United States," while also facing "ongoing racial, economic, and political crises as well as enduring violence (personal, cultural, and structural) that require us, if we were not already, to prioritize wellness in caring for a unit of human beings."

In her "What Do Department Chairs Do?" article, Evans asks one simple question: "How might we fundamentally reimagine the department chair role in a way that creates a new, more socially just normal?" Toward that end, we seek to inform those in upper administration about how to recruit and retain Black women for leadership positions, so that fewer of us will be *the only one* at the deans', provosts', and presidents' tables where decisions are made, and can bring our diverse experiences into the room with us. As part of the

Chair at the Table network's mission, we debunk the myth of limited availability of diverse candidates for administrative leadership. Black women are ready and willing to lead.

Dear Department Chair is our gift to the next generation of leaders, as we share our experiences in service to those who will certainly struggle but will hopefully move beyond the need to offer "condolences" for the position. Understanding the role of department chair is critical to understanding the entire university structure, and those without experience or intimate knowledge of this role should not be favored candidates in leadership roles that have the power to impact campus decision making that people in this role will be responsible for carrying out. Since department chair is the gateway administrative role, our emphasis is directed toward this pivotal juncture in one's professional trajectory. There is another way to experience this work—beyond the oppressive "boss" paradigm. Administrative work can be grounded in gratitude, support, kindness, and care. We hope these letters help future leaders find pathways to creating new, more equitable, and more humane norms for leadership.

References

Comiskey, James C. *How to Start, Expand & Sell a Business: The Complete Guidebook for Entrepreneurs.* San Jose, CA: Venture Perspectives Press, 1985.

Evans, Stephanie. "Guest Editors' Introduction: 'We've Been Lovers on a Mission.'" *Palimpsest: A Journal on Women, Gender, and the Black International* 10, no. 2 (2021): vi–xxi.

———. "Letters to Our Daughters: Black Women's Memoirs as Epistles of Human Rights, Healing, and Inner Peace." In *The Black Intellectual Tradition: African American Thought in the Twentieth Century*, edited by Derrick Alridge, Cornelius Bynam, and James Stewart, 100–126. Champaign, IL: University of Illinois Press, 2021.

———. "Meditations from a Black Woman Chair: Social Justice Values and a New Normal in Academic Administration." *The Department Chair* 32, no. 1 (Summer 2021): 12–15. https://doi.org/10.1002/dch.30395.

Stanley, Christine A., ed. *Faculty of Color: Teaching in Predominantly White Colleges and Universities.* Bolton, MA: Anker Publishing, 2006.

Thomas, Marlo, and Friends. *The Right Words at the Right Time.* New York: Atria Books, 2002.

Resources (Handbooks, Journals, Organizations)

- College/Institution Chair Professional Development and Academic Leadership Development Program
- *The Department Chair* (Journal, Wiley Publishing)
- *The Chronicle of Higher Education* and *Inside Higher Ed*
- Academic Chairpersons Conference (University of Kansas)
- HERS Leadership for Women
- Harvard University ACE Fellows Program
- Academic Impressions

Recommended Reading

- *Jossey-Bass Resources for Department Chairs*, including *Communication Strategies for Managing Conflict: A Guide for Academic Leaders* by Mary Lou Higgerson (2016); *Positive Academic Leadership: How to Stop Putting Out Fires and Start Making a Difference* by Jeffrey L. Buller (2013); *The Department Chair Primer: What Chairs Need to Know and Do to Make a Difference* by Don Chu (2012); *The Essential Department Chair: A Comprehensive Desk Reference, 2nd Edition*, by Jeffrey L. Buller (2012, 2006); *Time Management for Department Chairs* by Christian K. Hansen (2011); *Facilitating a Collegial Department in Higher Education: Strategies for Success* by Robert E. Cipriano (2011); *Department Chair Tool Kit Set* by Don Chu (2008); and *Engaging Departments: Moving Faculty Culture from Private to Public, Individual to Collective Focus for the Common Good* by Kevin Kecskes and Eugene Rice (2006)
- *The Department Chair Field Manual: A Primer for Academic Leadership* by Don Chu (2021)
- *A Toolkit for Department Chairs* by Jeffrey L. Buller and Robert E. Cipriano (2015)
- *The Department Chair as Transformative Diversity Leader: Building Inclusive Learning Environments in Higher Education* by Edna Chun, Alvin Evans, et al. (2015)
- *Working with Problem Faculty: A Six-Step Guide for Department Chairs* by R. Kent Crookston (2012)
- *The Essentials for New Department Chairs* (The Department Chair Book 21) by Carolyn Allard (2011)

- *Department Chair Leadership Skills* by Walter H. Gmelch and Val D. Miskin (2010)
- *The Academic Chair's Handbook* by Daniel W. Wheeler, Alan T. Seagren, et al. (2008)
- *The Department Chair's Role in Developing New Faculty into Teachers and Scholars* by Estela Mara Benisimon, Kelly Ward, et al. (2000)

Part I

Letters from the Chair

I

A Chair's Epistle

*Finding the Color Purple and Your
Leadership Identity in a Field of Email*

Tiffany Gilbert

Chair, University of North Carolina Wilmington

I write this letter to you, Sister-scholar, with abundant love and expectation for your success in this new role. You have probably received as many condolences as congratulations—academics can be so fantastically unoriginal sometimes—and may have a few trepidations of your own. With one vote, your status among your peers has shifted: *You* are in charge and entrusted with the department's future. You have read the university's faculty handbook, the department's policies, the contents of my flash drive. The list of chair duties is as complex and daunting as a car manual. Budget oversight, curriculum development, faculty and student support, even building supervision. *How will I get it all done?* you wonder anxiously.

Think about young Celie in Steven Spielberg's 1985 adaptation of Alice Walker's epistolary novel, *The Color Purple*. Becoming department chair for a Black woman academic, particularly at a predominately white institution (PWI), is akin to Celie's first morning in Mr. ___'s house: it involves organizing chaos you did not create in an institution not designed with you in mind. In the film, Celie scans the kitchen, appalled at the tableau of filth and neglect. The walls are slick with grease and soot, food waste and dirty dishes crowd every surface, and mice scurry freely along the baseboards. With only a bucket and a sponge, Celie gets to work. Spielberg captures her labors in a montage that tracks the gradual restoration of life and functionality to the derelict space. She scrubs the walls until a hopeful floral-patterned wallpaper emerges. Through her ingenuity, she jerry-rigs a pulley system to hang pots and pans until ready for use. She polishes flatware and fixtures to an impossible gleam and builds an inviting fire on the hearth. This order borne out of Celie's toil is short-lived, as the thud of an icy, muddy boot on the table heralds Mr. ___'s return from the fields. He is the boss of this patch of earth, and Celie exists—to invoke Zora Neale Hurston—as his mule. Sadly, this scene initiates the cycle of perpetual servitude in which Celie will spin, powerlessly, for most of her marriage.

Origin Story

I begin with this vignette from *The Color Purple* as an analogy for my astonishment at the scale and depth of the responsibilities I assumed on July 1, 2016, though it would be arrogant and unseemly to suggest that any aspect of the administrative role of department chair at a university is akin to the plight of Black women Alice Walker represents through the character of Celie. By dint of our credentials and profession, we possess an agency and autonomy that women like Celie could probably never envision, much less experience. We teach topics that provoke and sustain us; create communities among our students and peers; write from our hearts and rage about what matters to us, whether it be on divas and place, transnational conceptions of home, or Black historic preservation. We earn tenure with the tenacious verve our ancestors instilled in us. And, for many of us, we accomplish that goal and more under the watchful curiosity of senior colleagues or, more seriously, in the face of determined opposition.

Occupying positions of heightened visibility was nothing new to me: having graduated from three PWI institutions, I was quite accustomed to being one of a few students of color (if not the only one) in the room. When I joined UNCW's English Department in August 2006, I was hardly surprised that I was the only person of color on the tenure track. Wilmington, North Carolina is, as I recently reflected in another piece focused on leading a department during the pandemic, a fascinatingly ahistorical place, where the aftershocks of the 1898 white supremacist–organized massacre and insurrection continue to reverberate. Most obviously, the impact of the massacre is evident in the numbers of Black people living in Wilmington: while Black residents exceeded the number of Whites in 1890, they accounted for roughly 17.2 percent of the city's population in 2021, according to the US Census. My new colleagues acknowledged that, while there had been other Black tenure-track faculty in the past, there was never more than one at a time. All had left the university for various reasons, including for richer opportunities at other institutions or for a larger community of Black professionals with whom to socialize. Except for one five-year period in the late 2000s when another Black assistant professor was hired (she left after earning tenure), I was the only Black woman in the department until 2017.

Despite this unfortunate reality, my departmental life was, for the most part, genial and undramatic. To my colleagues' credit, I never felt that I could not express myself in my inimitable way; I owned my voice and was encouraged to use it. I succeeded in the classroom, where the majority of my students were white and where, occasionally, entire semesters would pass without any students of color on my rosters. Exceptional peer observations, positive student evaluations, and a cadre of students who registered for every class I taught confirmed that I had established my place in the department. Senior colleagues valued my scholarship, praised my writing, and offered perspectives from their research areas that often led to fascinating avenues of inquiry I had not considered. And, though I massaged my own doubts and imagined some rather ludicrous nightmare scenarios about the process, I secured tenure—with unanimous support all the way up the decision chain—in 2012.

Mid-Career Malaise

It did not take long for me to come down from the professional high of earning tenure, however. For the first time in almost two decades and across three degrees, I had no real insights about my next move. Without the tenure clock tolling incessantly in my head, I felt directionless. The classroom was becoming intellectually claustrophobic; frankly, playing the starring role as "professor of color" had started to wear on my nerves. Several monograph ideas percolated in my brain, but nothing compelling bubbled to the surface of my imagination, as I found most topics either creatively wanting or needlessly pedantic. Would the rest of my career stretch into years of yawning predictability? Teaching the same texts, repurposing time-worn notes? Others had trod this path to protect research time; I refused to become a fellow traveler. As a textbook Gemini, this kind of "autopilot" pedagogy did not sit well in my spirit. I had shape-shifted my scholarly identity before, during my doctoral studies at the University of Virginia (UVA). After completing coursework and passing oral comprehensive exams on nineteenth-century British literature, I abandoned it all to write a dissertation on the diva figure in mid-twentieth-century American film. Thus, unafraid to risk a relative degree of post-tenure tranquility, I sought a different experience. What that experience would be, I had yet to clarify.

Chairing in a Mad, Mad World

In my department, a "chair pipeline" did not exist. Ascertaining who would seek the position became a source of palace intrigue, so to speak, transforming what should be a simple procedural matter into grist for the gossip mill. So, when the opportunity arose to serve as chair for a one-year interim period, I stepped boldly into possibility and nominated myself. If anything, I thought, the interim gig would give me a taste of administration and a "behind the curtain" glimpse of the department's role in the broader university ecosystem; importantly, if I did not like it—or if my colleagues wanted to go in another direction—I had an exit. Six years on, the interim experiment appears to have succeeded: In March 2022, my colleagues voted unanimously to elect me to another three-year term.

Sister-scholar, chairing a department "ain't been no crystal stair." It requires a stunning degree of nimbleness and tolerance for chaos that no job description can convey. Apart from my interim year and first year as permanent chair, I have experienced only one "normal" semester in this role. Stephanie Y. Evans neatly lays out a chair's duties in a recent issue of *The Department Chair* newsletter. In two columns labeled "Tasks" and "Skills," she enumerates eleven categories that fall under the chair's purview. Such a schema visualizes what the job entails, yet it cannot prepare you for the apocalypses that have cycled through our university, the country, and the world. Consider this timeline. In September 2018, Hurricane Florence stalled over the Atlantic coast and devastated parts of UNCW's campus, the city of Wilmington, and wide swaths of the region surrounding New Hanover County. Faculty and students evacuated to safer locales, and the university shut down for a month. Though instruction came to a halt as well, administrators—from chairs to the chancellor—supervised their units from a distance. A month later, we returned to campus, clinging to the one fact that seemed immutable: winter was coming, and this hellish semester would soon be over (Crowe 2018).

We commenced the spring 2019 semester more exhausted than invigorated after the winter break. Even as they were finalizing syllabi, some colleagues in my department and across campus were still displaced from their homes, preoccupied with renovation costs, and overwhelmed with claims adjusters and contractors. In September 2019, roughly a year after Florence's devastation, the university preemptively suspended operations for a week when Hurricane Dorian grazed the coastline. Thankfully, Dorian was a minor event. In retrospect, it was the last gasp of normalcy, as the bottom fell out in 2020, when the coronavirus pandemic paralyzed the entire world. And, if natural disasters were not enough, the murder of George Floyd by police officer Derek Chauvin sent paroxysms of outrage across a quarantined America. Each of these events, catastrophic in its own way, has left a special signature on my chair tenure.

Leading a department is hard. It ain't no joke, to paraphrase 80s hip-hop emcee Rakim. The workload is inchoate, borderless. So, where does *The Color Purple* fit into this discussion? As we read Celie's letters to God, we become intimate not only with the daily travails she must carefully navigate to avoid piquing Mr. ___'s wrath but also with the sororal network she builds with Nettie, her blood sister, and with Shug and Sophia, women she later embraces as "sister-friends." All three women, in their inimitable way, encourage Celie to fight, not just to "stay alive" but to flower in an otherwise furious landscape. To acknowledge and, as Shug models, to claim the color purple as her own. I wish the same for you. While it may be possible to survive a chair term one spreadsheet at a time, outlasting the administrative onslaught and compassion fatigue with your spirit intact requires more than flashy Excel expertise. Here is what I have learned after six years in the chair.

FLEX YOUR VOICE

Throughout *The Color Purple*, Celie struggles to speak up and out either in fierce self-defense or from a place of desire. What does she want? Who does she want to be? Victimized by the man she believes is her father and forced to marry Mr. ___, Celie is beaten, shamed, and intimidated into silence. Not until much later in her adulthood, when she encounters Sophia and Shug, does Celie come to believe she is entitled to the voice her sister Nettie had tried to teach her to cultivate. As Black women academics, we often feel we cannot be our authentic selves in the classroom or the corner office. Preemptively, we may silence or otherwise contain our multitudes out of fear of real or tacit censure. As a result, we exist in our workspaces, in my reckoning, as "semi-presences"—there, but on guard, always at a remove. Bain et al. (2017) see this kind of bifurcated professional existence as toggling between two impulses, "masking" and "spill-outs":

> Masking and spill-outs are tools, employed consciously and otherwise, that help us to navigate the emotional terrain of neoliberalized academia. While spill-outs offer an outlet for the expression of a variety of feelings: excitement, joy, anxiety, self-doubt, or fatigue, for example, masking is often an act of self-preservation. Emotions that may be consequential to one's position or relationships in the academy, if expressed openly, are masked or hidden away, manifesting and usually spilling over elsewhere. Attending to the sites where spill-outs occur exposes the connectivity between our public (professional) and private (personal) selves.

On social media, hashtags like #BlackInTheIvoryTower and private groups like "Binders Full of Black Women and Black Nonbinary People in Academia" on Facebook provide Black women with a forum in which to narrativize their experiences and otherwise utter into existence the totality of their professional identities away from the surveillance of some White colleagues. The orchestrated opposition against Pulitzer Prize–winning journalist Nikole Hannah-Jones's application for tenure at the University of North Carolina crystallized for me the importance of expressing yourself and your values. I recognize that I have been enormously privileged to work within a unit and college that have given me space to cultivate my professional voice. I am also sensitive to the fact that this may not be case for other Black, Indigenous, and people of color (BIPOC), women of color (WOC), and women-identifying professors on our campus or at other institutions.

With this role comes the responsibility of advocating for the department, communicating disciplinary realities to the dean, for example, to justify new lines, programs, or resources. These conversations will test your diplomatic mettle, as you negotiate on behalf of your faculty, staff, and students. Other conversations will drain you, despite their importance. Since the murder of George Floyd in May 2020, UNCW has been in the middle of a reckoning. After a request from representatives of the Black Student Union to paint Black Lives Matter (BLM) messaging in high-visibility areas on campus, the chancellor retorted that "All lives matter," and the university was thrust into a public relations crisis (Gilbert 2022). Since then, UNCW has shifted into maximum overdrive to address the poor numbers of Black faculty on campus, as well as other substantive diversity, equity, and inclusion (DEI) issues. The College of Arts and Sciences embarked upon a cluster hire and established a standing committee on access, equity, and diversity (AED), which I co-chaired from 2020 to 2022. We know how much this kind of embodied service can affect Black women academics, that it can accelerate burnout, hinder progress toward promotion, and increase disillusionment. This is necessary work, nevertheless. If we remain silent, someone else will speak to advance their own cause. Our voice is our capital—we cannot afford silence.

CHAIR FOR THE CURRENT CONTEXT

Institutional memory can be an asset, but sometimes it cannot meet the challenges of the moment. Hurricanes and a global contagion forced us to become exhaustingly present. They have cleaved my chair experience into two distinct realities: the first half focused on learning and acclimatizing to the shift in my departmental identity; the second has been focused on recovery and survival. No one understands what it means to lead a department during a pandemic like the other members of your leadership cohort. The group of chairs and directors with whom I collaborate has provided perspective as well as solace.

However, given the extraordinary circumstances that have befallen UNCW since 2018, we could not simply rely upon institutional memory as a resource or comfort. Chairs and faculty alike, by necessity, had to rewrite the playbook, or, as a former dean put it on several occasions, to "build the plane while flying it." At the same time, we had to focus on the future of our respective departments and disciplines. Three weeks before Hurricane Florence's arrival, my English colleagues and I welcomed two new assistant professors. How would the interrupted semester impact their reappointment and tenure progress? How could we recover a "proper" working experience for them? These questions would inevitably overshadow the professional reality for three more hires whose first year at UNCW was largely virtual because of the pandemic.

Florence and COVID-19 were tectonic events that could not be anticipated. Other situations are bureaucratic in nature—changing administrations, byzantine business procedures, contrived metrics— and can further complicate basic tasks or simply interfere with the flow of an ordinary morning. Evolving "innovations" can prolong some managerial tasks and frequently require multiple calls to multiple units for clarification. In these instances, even my own earlier chair experiences couldn't really help. Lean on your chair cohort for advice, hacks, or space to vent.

Practice Humility

When I first presented myself to the whole department as a candidate for chair, the prospect of reciting or otherwise embodying my vita was not so important as introducing my colleagues to the origins of my values. Generations on both sides of the tree were faithful leaders in church and in other community circles. Growing up, I was a fortunate witness to and a beneficiary of their service ethic and stewardship in action. But as much as I have tried to lead with those values at the center of every decision, I have made mistakes. You will too. It is critical to own the missteps, promise to do better next time—and mean it. Remain open to alternative perspectives and be humble enough to adapt in the face of new information. It is not a sign of weakness to adjust viewpoints; not doing so can be interpreted as insecurity or intransigence.

Managing up and down, chairs occupy an administrative purgatory. We are often responsible for identifying solutions to problems that may make sense strategically but chafe our sensibilities as teachers. But, the weirdest thing about becoming chair is that, unless you are an external hire, you are selected from among your peers. Interpersonal dynamics inevitably become complex. There will be tears—some of them may be yours. Evaluating colleagues becomes more stressful as chair because you are the arbiter. The letters you write have an impact on reappointment, tenure, post-tenure review (RTP) decisions, grants, and awards. Any number of decisions can—and will—go sideways. How you honor the relationships among your colleagues will determine your success, regardless of your new position and title.

Protect Your Joy

Sugarcoating the truth about the demands of the department chair position will get us nowhere fast. It exacts an emotional and intellectual toll. You serve many masters, some of whom cannot agree on the color of grass. At the same time, you are positioned to influence the department's future in positive, consequential ways. Future-forward actions, like hiring new colleagues, bring their own kinds of drama and anxieties into departmental conversations. They must be managed with care and clarity. Since 2017, I have hired nine tenure-track professors and two lecturers. These faculty reflect the realities of our globalized society and evolving discipline. You will learn that making the case for faculty lines is complicated. It requires passionate advocacy, pragmatism, and diplomacy, especially when you meet with your dean, who likely will approach faculty line distribution with a different calculus in mind.

The small stuff can run amok like kudzu and take over your day. Checking the status of a classroom renovation with the college-level facilities coordinator, scheduling a meeting with your departmental steering committee, or mapping out new brochures to highlight curricula and travel grant opportunities for students: whatever it is, there never is enough time. The quotidian burdens of responsibility will obscure your view of the future, but it is there—beyond the overflowing inbox and endless meetings. Give yourself permission and time to be unavailable each week to take care of yourself and to maintain a fresh perspective on the department.

Let People Be

In my role, I have tried to abide by this classic chestnut: "You do you." Our scholarship may be the last outposts of academic freedom, as shining stars like Nikole Hannah-Jones and established paradigms like critical race theory are attacked in right-wing media and in other venues. Rev. William J. Barber has termed this era "the third reconstruction," echoing the period following the Civil War, during which white supremacist Democrats fomented fear and terror of free Blacks regaining control of the South. In this era of faux outrage, racial hate, and targeted misinformation, my colleagues have remained steadfast in their purpose. They are gifted teachers and mentors. They have designed creative initiatives that challenge students' perspectives, equip them with essential skills, and open many possible worlds for them. To support their work, I have endeavored to cultivate a community of trust, where faculty and staff can take risks and, in a fascinating and liberatory sense, "play."

To be explicit, I do not micromanage my faculty. That approach does not come naturally to me. I will concede that a rigorous managerial disposition may have a place in certain contexts, like piloting an airplane or performing major surgery, where there is no room for error. Running an academic department is not that sort of enterprise: there is space for invention and revision.

In my view, micromanagement radiates from a place of insecurity. It does not inspire confidence in a leader; at least, I have never been inspired by a micromanager. We can sense the differences between a leader and a tyrant. Celie cannot respect Mr. ___ because she fears him and the randomness with which he metes out violence for the pettiest of infractions. While our academic reality may not be as volatile—I hope—as the life Alice Walker crafted for Celie, it is not a stretch to imagine a chair who has misinterpreted the limits of her power. We have either been trapped in those departments or have heard the horror stories. How can my colleagues trust me to make the most optimal decisions on their behalf if I am profligate with authority? How can they thrive in our workplace if my reaction or approval becomes focalized to the point of resentment? The short answer: they cannot. Besides, maintaining that level of vigilance and scrutiny is tiring. Nobody has time for that.

Conclusion

I began this letter by invoking the housecleaning sequence in Spielberg's film interpretation of *The Color Purple*. By the time the film ends, Celie has escaped Mr. ___'s cruelty, opened a tailoring business, inherited the house and land that once belonged to her real father, and been reunited with her children and sister Nettie. Most significantly, she has secured her agency and voice within a matrix of systems determined to crush her will—capitalism, racism, patriarchy. The same systems function within the university industrial complex, broadly speaking. Still, the color purple is not out of reach, even if it is buried under an avalanche of email. Some days will seem like you are treading in cement and making negligible impact; others will be unexpectedly, fantastically gratifying. As you chart your course as department chair, claim your seat at the table. If you want to sing like Shug Avery, then sing. Take up space and leverage your voice.

For, like Celie, we are here.

References

Bain, Alison L., Rachael Baker, Nicole Laliberté, Alison Milan, William J. Payne, Léa Ravensbergen, and Dima Saad. "Emotional Masking and Spill-outs in the Neoliberalized University: A Feminist Geographic

Perspective on Mentorship." *Journal of Geography in Higher Education* 41, no. 4 (2017): 590–607.

Barber, William J. II. *The Third Reconstruction: How a Moral Movement Is Overcoming the Politics of Division and Fear*. Boston: Beacon Press, 2016.

Baxley, Traci Palmer. "Navigating as an African American Female Scholar: Catalysts and Barriers in Predominantly White Academia." *International Journal of Critical Pedagogy* 4, no. 1 (2012): 47–64.

Corbin, Nicola, William A. Smith, and Jose Roberto Garcia. "Trapped between Justified Anger and Being the Strong Black Woman: Black College Women Coping with Racial Battle Fatigue at Historically and Predominantly White Institutions." *International Journal of Qualitative Studies in Education* 31, no. 7 (2018): 626–43.

Crowe, Cailin. "Nearly One Month after Hurricane Florence, This Campus Is Still Picking up the Pieces." *Chronicle of Higher Education*, October 5, 2018. www.chronicle.com/article/nearly-one-month-after-hurricane -florence-this-campus-is-still-picking-up-the-pieces.

Evans, Stephanie Y. "Meditations from a Black Woman Chair: Social Justice Values and a New Normal in Academic Administration." *The Department Chair* 32, no. 1 (Summer 2021): 12–15. https://doi.org/10.1002/dch .30395.

Gilbert, Tiffany. "Chairing in the Pandemicene: Coronavirus, George Floyd, and the Year of Living Dangerously." In *Disaster Pedagogy for Higher Education: Research, Criticism, and Reflection*, edited by Victor Malo-Juvera and Nicholas C. Laudadio, 157–72. Lanham, MD: Rowman & Littlefield, 2022.

Lawson, Victoria. "Geographies of Care and Responsibility." *Annals of the Association of American Geographers* 97 (2007): 1–11.

Reed, Bryant. "Student Reacts to UNCW Chancellor 'All Lives Matter' Comment." *WECT News 6*, June 13, 2020. www.wect.com/2020/06/13/ student-reacts-uncw-chancellors-all-lives-matter-comment/.

Spielberg, Steven, dir. *The Color Purple*. 1985. Warner Bros. Pictures.

United States Census Bureau. "QuickFacts: Wilmington City, North Carolina." n.d. Accessed December 12, 2022. https://www.census.gov/ quickfacts/wilmingtoncitynorthcarolina.

Walker, Alice. *The Color Purple*. New York: Harcourt Brace Jovanovich, 1982.

WECT Staff. "UNCW Black Student Union Leaders 'Disappointed' by Chancellor's 'All Lives Matter' Comment during Meeting." *WECT*

News 6, June 12, 2020. www.wect.com/2020/06/12/uncw-black-student
-union-leaders-disappointed-by-chancellors-all-lives-matter-comment
-during-meeting/.

Winters, Mary Frances. *Black Fatigue: How Racism Erodes the Mind, Body, and Spirit.* Oakland, CA: Berrett-Koehler, 2021.

2

From Freedom to Liberty

I Am Not My Skin

APRIL LANGLEY

Chair, University of South Carolina

Herstory: Preparing for the Journey

It's been twenty years since I first came to the University of Missouri-Columbia—fresh out of grad school and a tad bit older than many of my colleagues in the English Department. I had always loved literature and especially African and African American authors. So, I was ecstatic when I received a tenure-track appointment in an English Department, with a specialization in Africana Literature, at an R1 institution. What I couldn't name then, but now understand, is that the work I was doing was always interdisciplinary and it didn't necessarily fit into a neat box. My teaching and research in early Afro-British American literature pre-1900 meant that I had to work hard to make my conference proposals, papers, articles, and of course my first book fit audiences that would rather read about contemporary African American and early Anglo-American works. As a result, I spent countless hours reading across disciplines (history, psychology, religion, gender studies, sociology, ethnography, art history, business, criminal justice, and Africana studies—to name a few) and across historical periods from the 1700s to 2000s. I found that I enjoyed teaching and researching and engaging in community work that fed my desire to center knowledge production, sharing, and dissemination in ways that centered Black cultures, societies, and histories. Consequently, nearly all the English Department courses I taught were cross listed with Black Studies, and I found myself designing and redesigning "traditional" literature and theory courses toward the goal of decentering limiting frameworks that privileged conventional ways of understanding "American" literatures.

Following my passion, I promised myself that when I earned tenure, one of my first projects would be to move half my academic line over to Black Studies. During my first five years, as an assistant professor, I became an affiliate of Black Studies and was so involved with the program that I was invited to many committees. Perhaps the most important one was the Black Studies Executive Committee, an advisory board that worked toward revising and researching the proposal for departmental status. Black Studies became an official department in the College of Arts and Science in 2013. This is one of the most fulfilling achievements of my career, being part of this legacy. While on this committee I met some of the strongest faculty and administrators—all affiliates—across campus from many disciplines. This community is still a strong support.

The Journey Begins

In my second year after earning tenure, I was asked by the current director of Black Studies to serve as interim while she was on leave. However, I deferred to the current assistant director and agreed to serve as interim assistant director instead. Let me pause here to say that this was not a decision I would make again. Looking back and without regret, I would have accepted the interim director position, but I lacked the necessary confidence to do that at the time.

> **Advice**: take the position and believe in yourself and call upon your support system for help to grow into a leadership position—at worse "fake it till you make it." Too many of us—Black women—are afraid to step up. And it's likely because we've been presumed incompetent for so long that we have lost faith in our own abilities.

That was me then, and, full disclosure, I was not able to simply "pull myself up and out" of the sunken place. It took another Black woman, who had been where I was afraid to go, to encourage me and let me know that this was where I was needed, and more importantly that I was more than able to handle the position. If not for her I might have missed an important point. That resistance begins with small acts that move us to places and spaces where we experience communal and personal healing as part of a larger project of social justice and the lifting of others—especially, but not only, those we serve as campus leaders. It is difficult to help others if we carry and believe the hype that devalues us. We often work twice as hard but, when opportunities come along, we don't step into that position for which we've been long preparing.

The Journey Continues: Pivoting Hats

After a year as assistant director of the Black Studies Program, a year spent learning and growing, working on revising the major, creating new courses and revamping a dated curriculum, as well as creating connections between "town and gown" that had not existed before, I felt confident in the position. So, I finally requested to move half my line over to Black Studies. I didn't know it at the time, but I would soon be offered a more permanent position, when the director returned from leave. She determined that I had done such a good job as interim that she wanted to work with me as assistant director. Two years later when we became a department, the assistant director position was eliminated.

I continued to function as a de facto director of undergrad studies, serving on all hiring committees and working with the chair to build our new department, while also serving as the literature coordinator for the English Department. This position in English meant working with graduate instructors and helping them prepare to teach lower-division survey and other literature courses. I held seminars and workshops and created training groups. When the Black Studies chair retired two years later, I continued to do the work I had been doing and was unable and felt unprepared to be department chair. During this time, I was a primary caregiver for my elderly mother, who had begun showing signs of dementia and who has subsequently been diagnosed with Alzheimer's. I simply did not have the where-withal to hold an administrative position and care for family.

> **Note to future self**: Know when to say when—and tap out if you need to—and feel good about your decision. There are times when the personal needs to be prioritized over the professional.

While at that time I felt guilty for not stepping up, in retrospect I'm glad I was able to recommend a colleague I greatly respected, who turned out to be the perfect person for the job. I should also add she was the person, that amazing sistah-doctah, who helped lift me out of the sunken place.

> **Note**: Always watch for people who have promise and talent; celebrate and move others along when you can. I really appre-ciate this about my journey—the many leaders I've met along the way who inspired and mentored me without even knowing it. They've taught me to do the same.

The Journey Back to Me—
Up from the Sunken Place

I continued to work with the new chair in the same way and watched our unit grow. I was at times a kind of "right-hand" person to whom she came for suggestions, and I learned a lot from her about serving. When she left the university to take a position at another institu-tion, she insisted that I run for chair, and she strongly advocated for me. During the voting process I was unsure but decided I would go for it. The department elected me, and the Dean confirmed it, and a year later as department chair, I was able to put forward the first faculty member for tenure in the Department of Black Studies—a difficult endeavor but a huge success. In December of this year, I was appointed interim chair of English (the first person of color to hold this position), and I simultaneously chaired two departments for six months, during one of the most difficult semesters in recent history.

As I reflect on my career trajectory thus far, it has been a somewhat uneven and challenging journey to this point, but it has taught me many lessons about what to do and what *not* to do.

Sitting in the Chair: Responsibilities, Challenges, and Rewards

As the chief academic and administrative officer of the Black Studies Department (BSD), my official responsibilities include but are not limited to exercising leadership in the following ways: implementing the mission of the BSD to develop quality teaching, research, and public service; coordinating academic planning; managing faculty and curriculum development; handling budget development and oversight; implementing human resource policies and decisions; and administering governance policies and procedures, as well as providing oversight for the daily responsibilities of a growing organization. I identified and appointed the first Director of Undergraduate Studies as a necessary role for the efficient and effective administration of the BSD. This position has been central to increasing our majors and minors, developing curriculum, and strengthening links between Black student organizations and the academic unit that supports them. Perhaps one of the unstated but most critical aspects of this position is measuring success by balancing student enrollment and faculty research. Because BSD is a small unit, much of our value to the institution and college is through our mission that supports and strengthens inclusive excellence in curriculum and programming as well as research.

Black Studies faculty are predominantly people of African descent. Their research and teaching encompass interdisciplinary and interconnected ways of bringing non-traditional work to traditional platforms. Therefore, the chair must watch carefully to promote and look for connections that can be made across a wide variety of interests, constituencies, and stakeholders. BSD has over thirty affiliate faculty from departments in the College of Arts and Science and other schools and colleges across the Mizzou campus (e.g., School of Journalism, College of Education, School of Health Professions, etc.). Annually, we administer Black History Month programming for the entire campus, as well as our departmental Fall Conference, and our Research Roundtables. BSD also regularly co-sponsors more than fifty events a year—both off and on campus. We have the distinction of being the only department to have hosted a sitting international or national dignitary/head of state—Prime Minister Andrew Holness.

In the past three years during my tenure, we have also hosted panels, symposia, and mini conferences, in person and virtually, with local political leaders from the state, as well as with distinguished international scholars. Our faculty have won several grants and awards, and we even have an award-winning staff person. For a chair of this type of academic unit, it is important to stay current and well-read in each affiliated discipline (to have at least a general knowledge, for example, of recent works in psychology, sociology, literature, history, and gender and sexuality studies).

Perhaps one of the more challenging (yet rewarding and necessary) tasks of chairing a department of Black Studies is *the internal work of inclusion, diversity, and equity* that is essential to avoid reinforcing historical "pockets of ignorance." It is a critical responsibility of leadership and management to "maintain department identity, environment, culture, representation, image, and morale" (Evans 12). To put it another way, chair work makes sure that this is not "your grandfather's Black Studies." It means attending to and striving for social justice as hard internally as externally. Consequently, it took two years to get half of our faculty to include their pronouns in communications, to attend safe space training, and to work against their xenophobic and United States–centric views of what "Black" is or "Ain't" when it came to curricular decisions. Even within a unit whose mission is critically engaged with the global work of inclusion and equity, it can take a concerted effort to bring faculty forward in their thinking about diversity. As a Black woman, I've found the challenges to be exacerbated by gender bias and presumptions about what a leader looks like.

A second related and equally vital task for a department chair is accountability to "local, national, and international communities" (Evans 12). As the liaison between upper administration and the department, and as one whose service is extended to multilayered and distinct communities, it is imperative to bring departmental issues, concerns, and achievements to the attention of administration—from within one's department to faculty councils and intercampus faculty cabinets, as well as other stakeholders and members of intra- and extra-campus and university communities. And, reciprocally, a chair must convey knowledge about interests, requests, requirements, and strategic plans from these diverse communities as well. Of course, this requires a chair to manage the inherent conflict that accompanies such tasks and responsibilities, per this process: "1. *Recognize* the nature and causes of conflict; 2. Identify and explore effective *response* options; and 3. Practice the art of principled conflict *resolution*" (Gmelch and Miskin 94). Indeed, conflict management is an indispensable skill for this position (Evans 12). As such, part of the job entails *educating faculty without alienating them*—walking a fine line between respecting faculty and staff freedom to think as they wish and modeling the kind of community that embodies the true inclusiveness about which we teach and that which our mission strives to achieve. The ability and, more importantly, the desire to work across race, class, and gender (across the spectrum) are strengths in this position.

A third vitally important task for department chairs is to *operate in transparent and fair ways* that ensure equity among all members of the department (faculty, staff, and students). Prioritizing and privileging *diversity, equity, and inclusion* in all aspects of one's work, in every task, is not easy, but it is paramount. This means that in all matters of department administration (e.g., fiscal, retention, recruitment, curriculum, etc.) a chair must operate in the best interest of the department and within guidelines of the institution (e.g., collected rules and regulations). However, I've realized more recently the value of "regeneration . . . retrospection . . . [and] introspection . . . to create an environment where everyone, especially historically oppressed people, can be well" (Evans 12–13). Pushing back against institutional structures that place unequal pressures and demands on Black faculty is as important as listening and hearing faculty who are struggling under these weights and constraints. Thus, the wellness of my department has become a principal guiding factor in most, if not all, of my responsibilities and tasks, and much of my work and efforts go toward holding myself, higher administration, and our department accountable to a level of wellness that extends beyond surviving to thriving.

My Recommendations

If I could offer some recommendations to the person that next sits in this seat, it would be these:

1. **"Seek first to understand and then be understood" (Covey 235).** To be sure, it can be frustrating to sit in meetings fraught with microaggressions and presumptions about our perceived incompetence—at departmental, college, campus, and university-wide meetings and discussion forums. We must remember, however, that it is important not only to hear but also to really listen to others. For one thing, we can gain a clearer vision of the field and of the obstacles or challenges we face by understanding the perspectives of those with whom we are most likely to disagree, and with whom we need to communicate to accomplish shared institutional goals. Furthermore, listening that leads to greater understanding can enable us to ask the kinds of questions that may permit people on different sides of an issue to engage in difficult dialogues.

   > **Note**: The clearest example of perspective-based hearing and seeing that I can recall is when I participated in faculty Difficult Dialogues training more than a decade ago at my university. Our instructor asked us to stand up and describe what we saw in front of us. Then, he asked us to face the rear of the room and do the same thing. Here's what I learned: Where you are and what you are looking for will determine how you "hear" or "see" another person's perspective and how they see and hear you.

   This enables us to build allies and bridges that will not only help mitigate some of the "blood pressure–raising" angst we experience, and deescalate our internal temperatures, but also provide valuable resources and partners for those we serve. I would add that at those times when we are neither able nor willing to "hear" from others, it's alright to take a time-out, refresh, and come back ready to listen.

2. **Learn from herstory.** That is, we don't have to reinvent the wheel every time. My mother used to say, "the worst of us can serve as a bad example"; we can learn from what works and what doesn't in our current environment. We can also learn by paying attention to what our intellectual foremothers have left as seeds to be planted for how we move forward despite obstacles. I regularly read a variety of sources on the history of Black women—especially those who have gone where I'm going. It doesn't all have to be "scholarly"—but I do recommend that scholars invest in a library of resources (books, blogs, music, poetry, podcasts, colloquia, conferences, etc.) to which you can turn for information, inspiration, and wellness. Of course, it is important to cite Black women and invite others to do the same. Anna Julia Cooper's life and work as well as Stephanie Y. Evans's *Black Women in the Ivory Tower* are my "go-to" herstories.

3. **Have a squad.** These are the people to whom you turn for advice, when you need to vent (where you can be an unapologetic angry Black woman), when you need a bit of "tough love" to determine whether the issue lies with someone else or with you. (Is this racism, sexism, etc. ism, or am I creating the problem?) Take care to nurture and appreciate your squad (which may consist of only one or two people you can trust without question) by always celebrating their successes and supporting them, as well as checking in with your own good news. Often this personal cohort of people are Black women leaders like yourself, but they need not be—sometimes they are mentors, family members, partners, and even allies. Trust is key here, and it may take a bit of work on your part to identify and locate your squad.

4. **Organize, strategize, and execute your administrative goals and responsibilities.** I've found it helpful to organize my work into categories and conduct weekly planning meetings with myself and then staff and faculty. I also create a strategic plan

for several larger short- and long-term goals I want to accomplish for the department, and then I create a timeline. I do this at the beginning of each semester—just before the semester begins. This way I have a guide to follow and a plan for executing and accomplishing my goals, and it's useful to consult when others ask for some of my time (with search committees, diversity work, and other institutional service). Once I've organized my administrative work, I can then organize my research and teaching as well. I've learned over the years that this kind of clarity helps me to reduce stress and to be better able to handle those "emergencies" and "fires" that we must put out—which always seem to come during our busiest seasons.

5. **Make and take time to "Sharpen the Saw."** This is habit seven of Stephen Covey's *The 7 Habits of Highly Effective People*: "It's preserving and enhancing the greatest asset you have—you. It's renewing the four dimensions of your nature—physical, spiritual, mental, and social/emotional" (288). This last recommendation comes from doing it wrong for so long that I am finally getting it right. You can't give what you don't have. Your own mental, emotional, and physical well-being is critical. Taking care of ourselves is probably the most important thing we can do. As Audre Lorde put it, "Overextending . . . is not stretching . . . Caring for [ourselves] is not self-indulgence, it is self-preservation, and that is an act of political warfare" (130). We can't possibly advocate for others if we don't care for ourselves. Seek a qualified therapist (even your squad can't handle it all), seek good legal counsel, develop a plan for health and wellness. Find things you love to do that bring you pleasure, pursue them, and make that part of your everyday life—privilege your own pleasure. Brittney Cooper and the Crunkfeminists have taught me a few good things in this regard.

Taking the Leap: Suggestions

Finally, I want to offer a few suggestions to those readers considering accepting the position of department chair. First, take some time to know yourself and really consider whom you will serve and to what end. Ask yourself the difficult questions that go beyond acknowledging your ability to do the job. You may be a stellar scholar with numerous accolades for your publications, you may have earned major grants and awards, but you also want to consider if you are the right person—at this moment—for this position and this constituency. I once suggested to a brilliant colleague that she consider a position as chair that our dean had announced. She promptly replied, "No way!" When I pressed, she admitted that while she knew she could do the job, and she felt a commitment to the mission of the academic unit, she had no desire to manage people. She was clear about her goals and, of equal importance, what type of work she was willing to do for the university. Perhaps you feel honored to have been asked by your dean, the current chair, or faculty in the department who value and respect your contributions and abilities. You might feel compelled to serve because there is a real need for women of color in this position—perhaps it's historical, perhaps you would be the first to serve in a role previously only occupied by white men or women. You may even have been offered quite a lucrative raise (to your base pay), with many other perks and opportunities for advancement and leadership beyond the chair's role. These are among the many reasons that people decide to serve. They are certainly fine reasons, but the first question you will want to consider for yourself is "Why?" What is your motivation?

The next important question is about timing. Is this the right time for me to accept this position—personally, professionally, or otherwise? I chose to decline the first opportunity to be chair because the timing wasn't right for personal reasons. You might, for example, need to consider your career trajectory and where you would like to be in, say, the next five or ten years. If, for example, you are at a research university, you might decide to delay an administrative position of this type until you have reached full rank or completed a significant research project. Or you may decide that this would be an excellent time to accept an administrative position in order to gain a broader perspective on your institution and begin building your professional steps to higher administration. Whether you are a new parent, an empty nester, caregiver for a parent, partner to a retiree, part of a joint faculty household, or in any number of other positions, your personal life will impact your decision about the best or right time to serve. Other determining factors include the scope, size, mission, and/or resources of the department, and your particular duties and responsibilities within it.

So, I suggest you seriously consider and even lay out a map for how your time will be spent. Consider accessing resources from higher education about the roles and responsibilities of a chair. You will also want to review internal documents, such as department, college, and university bylaws and collected rules that outline specific requirements of the position. You might want to survey current or and/or former chairs for more information about day-to-day operations, departmental cycles, and the most demanding and pressing issues. I also suggest scheduling a meeting with the dean to get feedback about your college's priorities and strategic plans. Yes, this is a bit of work, but it is well worth the time spent before—rather than after—you decide to accept, decline, or defer serving in this position to another time. Remember it need not always be a "yes" or "no" answer; sometimes the response is "not now, but I'd like to be considered for future appointments." Your careful deliberation about timing demonstrates the value and importance you place on this administrative service. After all, the transition from faculty member to department chair is a challenging one in the best of times, and even more so if you have not carefully planned or considered your timing.

Last, but certainly not least, I want to suggest that you spend time assessing two things: your fitness as this moment for this leadership position and your goals for the department. What strengths do I bring to this position? What additional training or learning would I need to be most effective in this position? And, related to the "why" question, what mark or contribution would I like to make to the legacy of this department's mission? Of course, you won't have fast and hard answers to these questions, but seeking the advice or input of others, perhaps more experienced leaders, will aid you in your decision. So, it will be important to research what support systems are in place and what national and international structures in your discipline you can look to for more information about substantive work that matters in this position. For example, as a chair of a Black Studies department in the SEC, I find the SEC Black Studies Association a valuable resource and place to convene with other chairs and directors about issues related to our interdisciplinary programs and departments. As a literary scholar, I also find sub-committees and forums of the MLA and CLA critical, as well as the AAUW, AAUP, ASALH, BWSA, NCBS, and of course Chair at the Table: Black Women & Academic Leadership Research Collective (chairatthetable.net/). National organizations can be extremely important for networking and sharing information among leaders in your areas.

Most important, don't forget to reach out to leaders and senior colleagues and peers, both inside and outside your institution, for advice, ideas, and even brainstorming. Find your chair mentoring squad, or a small group of administrators with whom you feel most comfortable, and they need not be at your institution. When you're at conferences or attending forums, take the time to network and listen. It is truly amazing what gems of collective knowledge and insights you can glean and contribute. You will also soon find yourself beginning to mentor others, and this is perhaps the most rewarding part of the journey from faculty to chair, as you begin to support and increase the pipeline of others like yourself.

In solidarity,
April Langley

References

Abrams, Stacey. *Lead from the Outside: How to Build Your Future and Make Real Change*. New York: Henry Holt and Company, 2018.

Cooper, Brittney C., Susana M. Morris, and Robin M. Boylorn. *The Crunk Feminist Collection*. New York: The Feminist Press at CUNY, 2016.

Covey, Stephen R. *The 7 Habits of Highly Effective People: Powerful Lessons in Personal Change*. New York: Simon & Schuster, 2020.

Evans, Stephanie Y. *Black Women in the Ivory Tower, 1850–1954: An Intellectual History*. Gainesville: University Press of Florida, 2008.

———. "Meditations from a Black Woman Chair: Social Justice Values and a New Normal in Academic Administration." *The Department Chair* 32, no. 1 (Summer 2021): 12–15. https://doi.org/10.1002/dch.30395.

Evans, Stephanie Y., et. al. Chair at the Table: Black Women & Academic Leadership Research Collective. https://chairatthetable.net/.

Gmelch, Walter H., and Val D. Miskin. *Leadership Skills for Department Chairs*. Madison, WI: Atwood Publishing, 2011.

hooks, bell. *Talking Back: Thinking Feminist, Thinking Black*. Boston: South End Press, 1989.

———. *Yearning: Race, Gender, and Cultural Politics*. Boston: South End Press, 1999.

Lorde, Audre. *A Burst of Light*. New York: Dover Publications, 1988.

———. *Sister Outsider: Essays and Speeches*. Berkeley, CA: Crossing Press, 1984.

Stone, Douglass, Bruce Patton, and Sheila Heen. *Difficult Conversations: How to Discuss What Matters Most*. New York: Penguin Group, 1999.

West, Traci C. *Wounds of the Spirit: Women, Violence, and Resistance Ethics*. New York: New York University Press, 1999.

3

Sisterhood Beyond Scholarship

Advice to a New Sister-Director

Janaka B. Lewis

Director, University of North Carolina-Chapel Hill

This piece is informed by advice passed between two Black women who worked together as scholars and colleagues. I've learned that even as we mentor each other in administration, we also draw from all of the moments of sisterhood and mentorship throughout our lives, from college to our years as colleagues. Beyond the study of Black women as engaged subjects, we also define and create our roles in administration, together.

At the November 2019 National Women's Studies Association Conference (the major conference in the field), I sat on a panel during the organization's Chairs and Directors portion to offer advice to new and incoming program and department leaders. Only two years into a directorship myself, of a Women's and Gender Studies program at a large state university in the mid-southern United States (a state that has definitely leaned more conservative in recent politics), I knew that some of the advice being given did not take into account what it meant to be a woman of color coming into a field that, although created by us, was not always welcoming to us. The question and answer session was helpful but general, as we thought about funding, state politics that influenced some of our programs and departments, and curricular and staffing issues. As a panel, we were not thinking about what it meant to hold each other as sisters in the field, and beyond that, what it means to be sisters within a discipline (in both literal and figurative senses).

Very soon after that panel, I sat on another panel with Black women that had been put together by my mentor-colleague on Black motherhood in academia: the conversation considered how to be activists, organizers, educators, and mothers at the same time. Questions came up about how to sustain ourselves while building up our children and our families. Both of these panels, and other conversations I engaged in during my time at the conference, lingered for me throughout the COVID-19 pandemic and its still under-discussed effects on academia. In the spring of 2021, as I prepared to transition out of my four-year term as director and officially pass the metaphorical light to my then mentor (who carried the position forward after my term), these conversations weighed on my mind, as I thought about how directorship requires not only collaboration but trust as well. This is, therefore, both advice to a new chair/director and also a sisterly conversation, as our conversations often go.

A Sisterly Letter

To My Sister in Scholarship and Now Administration,

Congratulations on taking the opportunity to explore another aspect of your skill set in this academic career. Assuming the additional responsibility when we already do so much as Black women (and during this continually tumultuous time) cannot be underestimated. There will not be much support in your transition. You might get a welcome note from senior administrators, but they won't tell you how to do this job. You will be connected to other program and department administrators and chairs who will offer their attention by email but will also be concerned with handling the same things you are and at the same times. Please be warned (although you already know) that you will be continually figuring things out on your own, despite the recruitment process that looked like support.

I was the only Black woman on our administrative council (the council of department chairs and program and center directors) in the college for a year after I began, and was perhaps the only one, period

(I was not in a space where I wanted to count). Soon after I began, I had the opportunity to play a role in hiring another Sister for department administration. The honest conversation I was able to have with her is one I won't forget, and we had the privilege to spend time together in meetings and separately conspiring on Black women's worldmaking from within. We also brought in a third Black woman who preceded both of us for years at the university, but whose experiences did not initially seem to line up with enduring through the leadership pathway (and yet she was a model for all of us). So, in three years (but after decades), Black women's administrative representation increased threefold. Although now back to two women administrators in the college, we saw the promise in change not because the institution did anything differently but because we chose to do it anyway.

I accepted my first campus leadership position as I earned tenure. At the time, I was the only Black woman program director but found a voice as a member of the Dean's Administrative Council in a community outside of the involved units. Further along in your career, with a forthcoming book and pending promotion, you already have the space to advise on college policies and procedures in addition to highlighting concerns of our unit. We now have the college's first Race and Social Justice Advocate, through a search that included a SEEDs Sister in hiring and one who was hired. This is how pipelines of inclusion work on all levels, not to mention our expanded ability to mentor Black women students who have gone into law, research, business, and health.

The privilege of our network, however, is that we often find what we need within our circles, and this network has bolstered me along my leadership journey. As we know, Black women come from and stand firmly within community in scholarship and in praxis throughout our careers. We also embody mentorship within our leadership praxis. When I attended Duke University for college, I found community in Black women's mentorship—from Dr. Martina Bryant, from a dean who was my college mentor and also from my Georgia hometown, and from educational administrators who saw in me possibly what they had once seen in themselves. My first Black Women's Studies professor, Dr. Charlotte Pierce-Baker (now retired from Vanderbilt University), taught me about what the field was and my inclusion in it. We also had a Black woman vice president, the only

Black woman I had met in a position of academic senior leadership at a predominately white institution (PWI). It was as apparent then as now that seeing representation across staff, faculty, and administrative leadership helps not just Black women but all members of the academic community to reach their greatest heights.

Before I entered the administrative pathway, I came into the tenure-track position with support of Black women scholars from my undergraduate and graduate fellowship, Mellon Mays Minority (now Mays) Undergraduate Fellowship (MMUF) and Graduate Initiatives Program (MMGIP). The woman who mentored me into my tenure-track position, also my Sister-scholar, throughout my early years at the institution helped cultivate relationships with me and other Black women mentees over meals and conversations. We grew this network based on informal gatherings, and in a *Feminist Wire* piece in 2013, we officially named it SEEDs (Sister Educators Eating Dinner(s)). SEEDs has expanded to include a listserv, a number of events, and, over the last few years, an in-person and virtual symposium on Black women and wellness. (In 2019, in response to a shooting on campus that took the lives of two students and traumatized the whole community, we held an in-person symposium; in 2020, as we struggled to find connection and continue or return to writing during the COVID-19 pandemic, we organized a virtual "writing to live" symposium.) We plant seeds of care for each other and make decisions in community. There is not a president or a board but instead a network of reachouts, a commitment to sharing information and ideas. New members are added through existing members, which increases all of our connectedness to each other. We continue to facilitate wellness and writing support, and we meet with incoming Sister-scholars and staff to provide networks of support in parenting, negotiating university concerns, and community building.

Sisterly Leadership

What I didn't realize at first (although I should have) is that a central expectation of this leadership role, as outlined in "The Chair: A Detailed Description" (Evans 2021), is to "Define/Support Institutional Goals AND to maintain safety" in a way that considers how well we care for each other. Conversation in administrative meetings often included who the chair is responsible to, and although, as Black women we may tend to think primarily of the care of our colleagues, the role of managing also involves reporting on how these goals, even the ones we don't create, are implemented. This means navigating policies and politics which sometimes do not make sense when input is not asked or channels of honest feedback are not available.

Another challenge of the role involves navigating climate complaints and conflict management. As chair or director, we are tasked with not only creating a climate but taking into account what the climate has been. If it has been toxic, we have to manage that toxicity by listening to multiple sides and deciding if and where to intervene. The conflicts we negotiate include those that were present before we came and that may be internal, external to higher administration, or even external to community. The way we do things is not just the way we want to but sometimes the way we have to in order to manage multiple perspectives. We identify the spaces that are not advanced enough to tolerate change even as we know our radical roots of transformation. And we decide how to make the overall climate better, one decision at a time.

In our case, the state (both the location and the state of politics) remains the same: we tried for years to secure a major in a discipline that challenged critical frameworks (and with the knowledge that some actively chose to ignore our impact). Fighting the endless battles to justify our existence despite the high visibility of our numbers and work made me tired, and I hoped that you would still want to continue the job. We are all tired after last year and the years before. This discipline does not always allow us to protect ourselves and conserve our energy in the way that we need to. Our students often require additional support for their own identities and interests, and we are usually happy to provide that through our teaching, mentorship, and programming. Unlike some other fields, our work is also our activism, which means that it can exhaust us even beyond logistical requirements of the position.

You, my mentor and Sister-scholar, will do things differently than I did. I stumbled through systems and was often preoccupied with other things—my research, my family, my place in general. I figured a lot out through networking, which is also one of your strengths. For peace and solace, even from paperwork, I came to rely on our village of Black women that we co-constructed for such times as these. As a senior scholar, you have been able to achieve so much in your career, and I fear the rigmarole of some aspects of the position will make it less "shiny" than it may have appeared. I know that you will set your goals and achieve them anyway.

A third point, though, involves how to care for yourself in a position that will not necessarily care for you. The broad scope of the position includes creating and managing curriculum, leading and supporting staff, maintaining the budget, and developing programming, and each of these aspects can seem like a full position in itself. We suffered major part-time faculty budget cuts in the past two years and, each time, having to go to hardworking faculty and help navigate reduced courseloads (and reduced funding) has been extremely difficult. In some cases, I was able to be creative and use external funding for courses, but each course lost had an impact on our program and on our students. Programming, however, has been a highlight, as we have been able to bring guest lecturers in to build and expand our community. During the COVID-19 pandemic, we took advantage of virtual opportunities to engage several Black and Brown scholars in thinking about a range of topics and concerns specifically around wellness and care. Leadership took the form of bringing people together to create sources of support for greater visions to be realized.

How can one person possibly manage what can feel like multiple positions, with the additional goal of caring for ourselves and each other in a way that isn't typical of the academy? The answer does not always come in a Standard Operating Procedure manual, and we are reminded that we don't always have to do things the way others did, but we can draw from their knowledge. Rather than just leaning in, we lean on.

LEANING ON OUR FOREMOTHERS

As a Black woman scholar of African American freedom narratives, I trace stories of Black women educators back to the nineteenth century, including Frances Ellen Watkins Harper (Maryland), Anna Julia

Cooper (North Carolina and Washington, DC), Lucy Craft Laney (Augusta, Georgia), and Charlotte Forten Grimke (whose educational journey took her from Philadelphia to Salem, Massachusetts; to Sea Islands, South Carolina; and back north). In addition to the work they contributed to established institutions after winning their freedom from slavery (or, in Forten's case, being part of the Black middle class in Philadelphia but not feeling free), these women also played a role in founding their own institutions. Both Lucy Craft Laney and Ellen Craft, whose husband William wrote about their narrative of escape in *Running a Thousand Miles to Freedom*, founded schools in Georgia. These women and others used radical leadership and creativity to create opportunities for themselves and their communities.

For my Sisters in the pipeline of administration, it will take radical leadership lessons learned from the nineteenth century, the civil rights movement, Black Power, and beyond to address the immense effects of systematic oppressions within academia. It will also take courage—of leaders, institutions, and governing systems—to promote and pursue the academic freedom our students deserve. I have learned that beyond being firsts (in units, in colleges, and at times even in universities), we can never let go of each other. Our mentorship matters, our connections matter, our health and sustainability in doing the work on behalf of ourselves and each other does as well. We need allyship and accompliceship with others, but we also need to continue to bolster ourselves in leadership positions, in community. More than just sitting at tables, we need to continue to command and demand space and to bring our Sisters along.

Although I did not feel ready for leadership at the time, I took the position as director as my tenure as associate professor was being confirmed, because I wanted the opportunity to grow and to develop what I wanted to see in a Women's and Gender Studies program—one that includes Black, Brown, and Indigenous folks, trans and queer folks, and younger as well as more senior faculty members. I was able to accomplish this by allocating part-time funds and even expanding alumni development opportunities to support additional hiring. I used program and grant funding to bring in speakers on Black women and care, wellness, and technological innovations, and I collaborated with Sister-scholars in other units to create greater access to these opportunities.

Carrying the Mantle

As we continue the traditions of leadership established by those before us while crafting our own paths and spaces in administration, my five recommendations are these: 1. Be who you already are in this space. It should not take more than you are willing to give. 2. Listen to others but allow yourself to learn your own ways to navigate the position. Your story does not have to be like ours, but lessons may be important. 3. Know when you are giving too much—of your time, your energy, yourself. We are often told to think of service as twenty or thirty percent of our total profile, when we know that it can likely take one hundred percent. Protect yourself first. 4. Don't accept the way that things have always been done just because. The budget has been an example for me, as initially I allocated it the way it had previously been done without change but then understood how to expand allocation in a purposeful way. I came to use it to hire Black and Brown and trans and queer part-time faculty; even though we did not have lines for full-time, we were able to enhance our curriculum and create possibilities for expansive inquiry. 5. Imagine and grow the program or department that you want to see. This takes steps, but do one thing at a time to make your vision real. Remember the sisterhoods that already imagined us here, the creative collectives that have been part of much of our historical labor. And finally, remember that the collective of care extends into administrative positions, too.

References

Evans, Stephanie Y. "Meditations from a Black Woman Chair: Social Justice Values and a New Normal in Academic Administration." *The Department Chair* 32, no. 1 (Summer 2021): 12–15. https://doi.org/10.1002/dch.30395.

Lewis, Janaka B. "Radical Leadership and Creativity: Race, Gender, and Academic Freedom." In *Academic Freedom: Autonomy, Challenges and Conformation*, edited by Robert Ceglie and Sherwood Thompson, 161–71. Bingley, UK: Emerald Publishing, 2021.

Thompson, Sherwood, and Pam Parry, eds. *Coping with Gender Inequities: Critical Conversations of Women Faculty*. Lanham, MD: Rowman & Littlefield, 2017.

4

Leadership at the Community College

Supporting and Celebrating the Diversity of Community

SANDRA JOWERS-BARBER

Division Director, University of the District of
Columbia Community College

Dear Division Director,

My return to academia began on my fifty-first birthday. On that day, January 15th, I sat on campus at Howard University, my alma mater, and took the graduate school writing exam. By age fifty-five, I had my PhD. I share my experience in every meeting with students so they can see that age does not have to be a deterrent to accomplishing a goal. I share this so they can understand that Black women have historically ignored any imposed time limits on their desire to achieve, gain new knowledge, master a new discipline, or earn a degree. (Evans 2008).

After obtaining my degree, I began teaching at the University of the District of Columbia located in Washington, DC. This urban land grant institution was established in 1976 to serve the residents of the District of Columbia. The university offers residents training in workforce development, associate degrees, baccalaureate degrees, and master's and doctorates. A major feature of the university is its community college. Students can obtain the AA or AS degree while taking the first two years of courses toward a BA or BS at the university. They can continue to work toward a master's or doctorate.

The diversity in the classroom was as energizing as it was challenging. My students were recent high school graduates, transfer students, veterans, single and married parents, returning citizens, and current and former members of the workforce. They had different reasons for being in the classroom but the end goal, to gain knowledge whether academic or workforce-related, was a shared one. I enjoyed teaching and I was happy to serve as an example that age was not a barrier to achieving an educational goal. Older students, I found, brought purpose and intention to the classroom. Several shared how their first experiences as college students had been interrupted by life events. Some started families, while others started jobs and careers. Many became the primary support for aging parents or siblings. Few of these life events allowed for the flexibility needed to continue to attend classes regularly. The university had evening classes but many did not meet the needs of unstable working schedules. Students who had weekends free found that there were few, if any, weekend classes. Students with computer skills who wanted to take classes online found few, if any, academic courses offered online. Left with no options, those students stopped attending classes, withdrew, dropped out. Later, when children grew up and became less dependent, when the role of caregiver ended and work schedules were no longer an issue, many returned to the classroom. I shared my experiences as an older, married-with-children student returning to school. Some of our issues were similar and many remained in place. We had class discussions on the challenges and benefits of being a working, older student who had been out of school for a while. The continued lack of class schedules that reflected the real-life situations of students was impacting student completion. They noted there was not enough variety in the evening classes and too few weekend classes. There were even fewer online classes and opportunities to meet with advisors or go to the registrar or other offices because they closed before the students could get to campus.

I realized during these discussions that I wanted to be in a position to act on such concerns. I wanted the ability to make change and shape policy. To me, becoming a department chair was the first step to making change. Learning what I needed to do to prepare myself for the position was critical. I met with my department chair and explained that I wanted to become more of an advocate for students on the administrative side. She was gracious and encouraging in her response to my request for training on being a chair. We decided that I would shadow her when I was not teaching. At our first meeting I came prepared, as requested, with data from the student surveys that noted their major concerns. I believed it was not divisive to acknowledge the situation and create a class schedule that better addressed the needs of working students. The data from those surveys supported the need for a different scheduling pattern. It also supported proposals for new course offerings. Each meeting was an educational awakening to what a chair did, when they did it, and why. The reasons why certain classes were only offered during the fall or spring semesters became clear. I learned how to use prior semester class enrollment data to determine which time slots attracted the most students. I was shown how to manually enter class schedules and faculty information into our Banner system. I then understood why the chair would be the last person in the office before each semester began. The mechanics of being a chair were more time-consuming and repetitive than I imagined.

Learning the budget process was the most challenging aspect of shadowing my chair. The funds allocated for the department were disbursed to the various programs within the department. I quickly learned that funding was not divided equally among programs. That was understandable, as some programs needed to prepare for external accreditation and others needed equipment. Getting funding and spending it were areas that needed constant attention and focus. Additionally, hard questions had to be asked and answered. Were STEM programs more deserving of a larger pool of money than the Humanities? Which projects would be funded if there were only a certain number that could receive monies? How do you support faculty requests that are clearly not eligible for funding? I learned that not all good projects would be supported. I learned how to use problem-solving strategies when program requests for budget expenditures could not be granted. Working across disciplines and collaboration with other programs was essential. Once I understood that budget issues would always be a struggle, I started to investigate how other programs looked for external funding. Even more critical was getting funding for new full-time faculty. The negotiations with the dean that I saw my chair engage in were strategic, informative, and sometimes successful.

As part of shadowing my chair, I sat in when she was out of the office for several days. It was during this substitution that I experienced some of the demands and pressure put on the chair by faculty, students, and other chairs. I was told that I had received good reviews from faculty and the dean when I sat in for the chair. I was encouraged that I now understood how to handle a budget, write proposals, enter data into Banner, and use data to support new projects. I learned how to use roll-over enrollment to determine the best times for courses and when to experiment with a new course placement. I learned the art of equity class placement and the importance of balancing day and evening courses. But the most important lesson was seeing my chair modeling ethical, equitable, consistent, and transparent decision-making. At times it was overwhelming, but I loved it all (Urtel, Smith, and Jowers-Barber 2018).

When the director of the history program stepped down, I was encouraged to apply for the position. I knew that I was ready and I was selected to serve. It was a short appointment that came at an institutional academic low point. After a year of discussion about the need to close low-performing programs, the university acted. History was one of seventeen programs that were shut down. My argument that the history program at an HBCU (Historically Black College and University) was critical to the identity and culture of the institution was unsuccessful. The number of graduates from the program and the number of students enrolled were too small for it to survive. The reality of the limitations of a chair hit me hard. At least some history courses would continue to be offered at the university's community college. This college had previously been housed on the university's campus and was now located in another part of the city.

When the history program at the university closed, a position for a director of the Humanities and Criminology Division at the community college became available. While the title is different, the responsibilities of the division director are equivalent to those of a chair. Because my chair had afforded me the opportunity to shadow her, to learn and perform most of the functions of a chair, I felt that I was qualified. My teaching, service, and professional development evaluations were excellent, and I had consistently strong student evaluations. I was ready for this new chapter in my academic career.

The population of the community college is composed of students who are often bringing years of life and work experience into the classroom. They are determined and focused. Many are in the workforce and are seeking enhancement of their skills in order to advance in their careers. Others are themselves supervisors and department heads looking to hone skills necessary to provide support for their teams. Additionally, there are traditional students coming directly from high school as well as transfer students. Some students are caregivers of parents or other family members. Many are parents themselves, raising young families. A number of students are returning to complete an interrupted journey. Some are enrolled just to stay current in a discipline and enjoy the intellectual engagement and social interaction.

The community college is intentionally student-centered and job market data–driven. Students come seeking degree programs that will provide employment in robust job markets. Older students bring a desire to finish in the shortest amount of time without any scheduling challenges that may impact their time frames. It is imperative for administrators to know what is happening in the local and regional job markets. The college must offer courses that align with the needs of the workplace. It is important to be informed about the realities of what the degree will mean economically to students. I appreciate and value the ability to quickly pilot new initiatives and best practices that address these issues. The Humanities and Criminology Division offers an Applied Associate of Science (AAS) degree and an Associate of Arts degree (AA). They are offered in four programs: liberal studies, law enforcement, legal assistant, and corrections administration. These program reviews require including external stakeholders to ensure that career competencies are being met. There is an emphasis on internships and experiential learning opportunities for students.

As division director I want to provide inspiration for the diverse student population. Important goals concern student retention, persistence, and completion. That requires understanding who the students are and what they want to accomplish. Mentoring students is necessary and rewarding. I meet regularly with students who want to know what a historian does besides teach. Many are still searching for their path. For students returning after a long time away from the classroom, there is a concern about their age. The belief that new technology and older students are not compatible is something we constantly need to address. Making technology accessible for students is critical, including providing online training throughout the semester so students can sharpen their skills without the limitations of work hours or other obligations.

Faculty who want to teach at a community college must bring passion, energy, and respect for the diverse student population. Teaching is the primary focus at a community college, and the ability to teach broadly and with depth is important. Every semester faculty provide assessments of their classes and student progress. These assessments are reviewed and used to inform course changes. Although research and publishing are not always linked to community college faculty, I support and encourage both. It is important not to think of the community college differently when it comes to these pursuits. Faculty should be supported in finding space for themselves in the arenas of teaching, service, research, and publication, and faculty and students encouraged to write on issues they discuss in class such as gender, anti-racism, and feminism. These and other topics have been addressed by Black women scholars without regard to an institution (Evans-Winters and Love 2015).

When I started as director at the beginning of the spring semester, budgets had already been set. Faculty had been assigned classes and division projects were identified. However, I found that the budget expectations for the division had not been met, and as director, I had to explain to faculty what happened. Having to defend a budget allocation that I inherited was new and difficult. Because I embrace an inclusive leadership style that combines service and leadership, I quickly met with faculty to discuss the reality of our budget and their expectations. I met with the full-time faculty and had them tell me what their budget hopes and expectations had been. I presented our reality and together we identified the top priorities of the program and began planning for the next budget cycle.

I do wish that I had been more aware of the tension around adjunct faculty–assigned courses. One of my first major assignments was to review all adjunct faculty credentials for alignment with assigned courses. I had the largest number of adjunct faculty in the college and this was a major effort. If I found that faculty were teaching courses without the proper credentials, I had to make the necessary adjustments. Some faculty would continue to teach their courses and others would be re-assigned courses or not assigned any courses. Although I thought that I was professional, collegiate, diplomatic, and tactful throughout this process, not everyone felt that way. The resulting uproar from faculty who had been let go was quick and ugly. My dean was supportive and fully available for me when I needed to talk. The situation was not pleasant but it had to happen. It was clear that, as director, this was part of the job that I'd accepted. Even when challenged I held open and honest conversations with faculty about the reasons their teaching assignments had changed or were ended. It didn't always eliminate hurt feelings, but it did foster an environment of transparency. While negative comments were part of the response, a consistent positive one was that "she listened to me." Through a stressful period, that feedback sustained me and encouraged me to remain as director.

Washington, DC, is a perfect location for academia. The numerous national historical institutions, landmarks, museums, monuments, and libraries make it an inspiring and accessible teaching laboratory. When I started teaching, I introduced the then relatively new discipline of public history to my history classes. Public history is intentional in its mission to teach and educate about historical events and actors in public settings. Monuments, memorials, historic preservation sites, statues, museums, and repositories are examples of public history sites. They can also be street signs, neighborhood churches, and houses. Writing assignments like reflective papers on visits to museums could be challenging for students whose work hours did not align with the traditional opening and closing hours of most museums. Expanding the assignments to include all public history sites allowed working students to visit a variety of sites. This provided flexibility and ultimately proved to be successful with all students. Students in classes outside of the division began telling their friends about "history in the streets." I shared with my colleagues how public history could be incorporated into almost every discipline. Students were encouraged to submit reflection papers with images of historical figures or selfies taken on the grounds and steps of historical sites. They could go on the weekend and take their families. This addressed some of the concerns of work schedules being a barrier to completing assignments, and it embodied the kind of the impact I envisioned making as chair.

I embrace a leadership perspective that values the contributions of all faculty. Since our division has the fewest number of full-time faculty and the largest number of adjunct faculty, we need to provide meaningful and relevant professional development for a diverse group. Faculty are encouraged to try new ideas and approaches to teaching. Workshops on enhancing teaching skills and increasing technology skills are offered throughout the year.

Division meetings are held twice a semester, with the most pressing issues prioritized and discussed, and teams formed to address them. Faculty meet more frequently to discuss best practices in teaching. They are encouraged and supported if they want to pilot a new course. Data collected from the pilot courses are reviewed with faculty, myself, and the dean. A decision is then made if the new course will be sent forward for approval by the faculty senate.

I provide space for conversations on how perceptions of age and race as barriers to academic achievement can be overcome. I speak with many older women students, who share their concerns about returning to complete their education. Many interrupted their academic journeys in higher education at a time when they did not see many women faculty of color in their classrooms. Students describe experiencing negative comments on their abilities from teachers who viewed their age, race, or ethnicity as handicaps to achievement. Unfortunately, the belief that, after President Obama's election, there would be a lasting newfound respect for and new thinking about minorities in education has not proved true (Harushimana, Alfred, and Davis 2019).

As a public historian, I understand that history is best learned when students can talk with individuals who were part of historical events and walk on sites where events took place. It is more impactful when they experience the places where historical actors lived and worked. To provide that experience, I ask that faculty include public history in some form in their courses, whether that involves student visits to particular sites or engagement with wonderful scholars and authors willing to speak to students about their research. When faculty report that students say "nothing important happened" where they live, I eagerly provide them names and contact information of individuals familiar with the city's social history, who look forward to speaking and sharing history with students. Students share stories told to them by their grandparents and great-grandparents about their life in the District. Students hear stories of domestic work in the homes of wealthy white District residents in the mid-twentieth century, and I provide context about the importance of domestic work for Black women in Washington in contributing to financial independence (Clark-Lewis 1996). A popular course on the history of Washington, DC, covers information about influential women of color and uses public history sites as a teaching tool. The English department identifies texts on local activists that align with public history site visits (Jones 2013). All faculty are helped in identifying local DC sites as part of their public history course components.

I am most proud of the New York City public history trip that has become part of our community college culture. The trips take place twice during the academic year, in fall and spring. These site visits include the African Burial Ground in Lower Manhattan, the United Nations, the Schomburg Center for Research in Black Culture, and a walking tour of Harlem. The African Burial Ground (open year-round) is the focus of the trip. Students also have the opportunity to visit the Schomburg and have personal time to shop and explore 125th Street in Harlem. Before the end of the semester in which they traveled, students submit one-page reflection papers. Their papers are amazing. The information they discover on enslavement in the North and in the city of New York shocks them. Some of the most moving reflections discuss the libation I conduct at the outdoor African Burial Ground memorial. Students are encouraged to include the names of their relatives during the libation ceremony. Reading these reflections about the trip reinforces the importance of providing students with opportunities to travel and view historical sites and have fun. Interestingly, a lot of our female students have expressed an interest in becoming historians, and it seems that previously, many thought only men became historians. The trip provides opportunities to show how women as well as men can participate in the field of history (White 2008).

The pandemic has taught me to be more forgiving of myself and others as I continue to grow as a leader. I have taken steps to attend more leadership conferences for my own professional development, and the concept of mindfulness has moved to the top of my self-care agenda. I have reclaimed my time on the weekends, though I do read and answer some emails on Saturday and Sunday. I take my allocated sick days before I get sick. I have embraced remote work and am able to conduct productive and concise virtual meetings. I have given myself and others the gift of grace; I understand that being a director is what I do and not who I am.

As I embrace the concept of servant leadership, I'm grounded by this quote from Maya Angelou: "I've learned that people will forget what you said, people will forget what you did, but people will never forget how you made them feel." As a leader who serves, I want people to feel that I listen to them when they discuss their issues. As a leader who acts, I want people to understand that their success is critical and I am dedicated to supporting them in accomplishing their goals.

Five Recommendations to Grow and Retain Effective Leaders

When growing leaders, it is imperative to emphasize that the desire to serve must be as compelling as the desire to lead.

Time must be provided for leaders to take advantage of regular professional development opportunities. Support should be given for projects that will enhance pathways for students to succeed. That same space will also support faculty projects and desire for advancement. The space can be a semester mini-sabbatical or an extended holiday break.

As this year of leading in the pandemic made clear, there must be more of an intentional emphasis on offering multiple means toward self-care with a focus on mental health awareness. It is time for a disruption in the ongoing and seemingly never-ending cycle of required program reviews, accreditation timetables, and eternal curriculum schedule postings.

Leaders will be productive no matter the location, but embrace the fact that the way work is done and where it is done has forever changed. Being able to work remotely can be re-invigorating. Deadlines can be met and issues addressed outside of a traditional office.

Holistic evaluations need to be in place for division directors to allow them to see how they are doing. They need to know the areas where improvement is needed. Most importantly, they need to know where they are excelling.

References

Clark-Lewis, Elizabeth. *Living In, Living Out: African American Domestics in Washington, DC, 1910–1940.* Washington, DC: Smithsonian Books, 1996.

Evans, Stephanie Y. *Black Women in the Ivory Tower, 1850–1954: An Intellectual History.* Gainesville: University Press of Florida, 2008.

Evans-Winters, Venus, and Bettina L. Love, eds. *Black Feminism in Education: Black Women Speak Back, Up and Out.* New York: Peter Lang Publishing, 2015.

Harushimana, Immaculée, Mary Alfred, and R. Deborah Davis, eds. *A Paradise to Regain: Post-Obama Insights from Women Educators of the Black Diaspora.* Gorham, ME: Myers Education Press, 2019.

Jones, Ida E. *Mary McLeod Bethune in Washington: Activism and Education in Logan Circle.* Charleston, SC: The History Press, 2013.

McGuire, Saundra Yancy. *Teach Students How to Learn: Strategies You Can Incorporate into Any Course to Improve Student Metacognition, Study Skills, and Motivation.* With Stephanie McGuire. Sterling, VA: Stylus Publishing, 2015.

Urtel, Mark, Stacey L. Smith, and Sandra Jowers-Barber. 2018. "Linking New Chair Preparation with First-Year Success." *The Department Chair* 28, no. 4 (Spring 2018): 18–19.

White, Deborah Gray, ed. *Telling Histories: Black Women Historians in the Ivory Tower.* Chapel Hill: University of North Carolina Press, 2008.

5

"Holding Sheshelf Together"

Citizenship of Feelings and Living Your Sacred Self

JULIA S. JORDAN-ZACHERY

Chair, Wake Forest University

Dear Department Chair:

Before I get into notions of citizenship and self-articulation, the point of this letter, I'll pause to introduce myself. I'm Julia Jordan-Zachery. I write this letter to you from my perspective as a quirky Black girl who grew up to become a chair of an academic department. I like to think of myself as a Black woman immigrant raised on the lyrics of Bob Marley—for me, "Exodus" will always resonate. As a little girl, I didn't fully comprehend the lyrics: "Rule equality/ Wipe away transgression/Set the/captives free." The understanding I gained as I grew older has influenced how I approach my role as chair. My socialization, which included a steady diet of Marley and others, helped me to practice "harm reduction and restorative justice" (Evans 2021, 14).

Now, let's talk about being chair and what that has meant for this quirky Black woman. My view of quirky is different from how Issa Rae, for example, understands it in her TV show *Insecure*—socially awkward, nerdy (although truth be told, I am a bit of a nerd, and I consider that a cool element of who I am). Instead, I'm understanding quirky in the sense that I tend to walk to my own beat, loving what I love, and feeling, and deeply, whatever it is I feel. To borrow from Janelle Monae, when I imagine myself as quirky, "I'm always left of center, and that's right where I belong/I'm the random minor note you hear in major songs," and guess what, "I like that." But this letter is less about me and my sense of self and more about how identity matters in relation to being an academic chair.

Osler and Starkey offer a typology of citizenship of which citizenship of feelings is a part. Citizenship of feelings is "a feeling of belonging to a community" (Osler and Starkey 2005, 11). Black feminists have long focused on belonging and on how identity influences one's feelings of belonging to multiple communities simultaneously. Audre Lorde, who often conceptualized her status as "outsider"—asserting her Black, woman, lesbian identity—is one example of how Black women have made themselves legible across multiple communities.

Using Osler and Starkey's notion of citizenship, alongside Black feminist thought, I explore the sacred self and its relationship to the role of chair. More particularly, I rely on Lorde's understanding of feelings—her use of feelings to critique the notions of citizenship and belonging while asserting her identity. Lorde writes, "all I had was the sense that I had to hold on to these feelings and that I had to air them in some way" (1984, 88). Feelings provide access to a knowledge that is "that dark and true depth which understanding serves, waits upon, and makes accessible through language to ourselves and others" (68). So, I want to bring together Osler and Starkey's understanding of the citizenship of feelings and Lorde's understanding of the use of feelings to talk about how one can maintain a sacred sense of self while being chair and across the process of performing the multiple tasks described by Evans (2021). I focus on you, the individual, you in community with members of the department, particularly Black male members of the department, and you in community with the college/university at large. I want to help you to engage in "[d]ecision-making that is ethical, equitable, consistent, and transparent," while also managing your stress levels (Evans, 14).

* * *

Let's enter into your sacred self. You already know this, but I'll repeat it—identity matters. As a Black woman in the academy, I face(d) many exclusionary practices. I talk about some of these experiences in the article "Licking Salt" (2019) and have had to work hard to find my way back from this. While this may not be particularly unique to the position of chair, I would argue it is even more relevant given that I was often the only one with my social location who entered meetings and other spaces. Being the only one can be a lonely existence and a painful experience (see Jones 2013). Having a clear sense of self is helpful for navigating these spaces. As we were seated around the roundtable one time, with various individuals sharing their opinions, I entered the conversation only to be interrupted by a white woman. Others had spoken, and no one interrupted them. But before I could utter a complete sentence, I was corrected. I leaned into the table, looked at the woman, and said, "I am speaking." I continued, only to be interrupted again. At this point I paused and said, "Once I'm done speaking, please feel free to respond."

You may find yourself in similar situations where some receive latitude and grace while systematically denying it to you. I refuse to call these incidents "microaggressions." Why? They are not micro in my experience, in the sense that there is often a consistent and pervasive pattern to them. The term "aggression" takes away the element of power that underlies such exchanges—racialized and gendered power. And truth be told, these types of exchanges hurt; they can drain our energies and, as a result, take us away from the work that we would like to do. Thus, it is so crucial that you boldly sit in your sacred self—that place where you know your truth and where you access your feelings and the knowledge they offer—doing this lets you define how you want to be a citizen and engage the role of chair.

To help us think through this notion of sacred self and citizenship of feelings, I turn to the short story "Blossom, Priestess of Oya, Goddess of Winds, Storms and Waterfalls," in Dionne Brand's *Sans Souci and Other Stories* ([1988] 1989). Blossom immigrated from Trinidad to Canada, where she married an abusive man and worked a series of dead-end jobs. Given the totality of her experiences, Blossom has a moment where she seemingly breaks down—she is crying and screaming in the street.

Next thing Blossom know, she running Victor down
Vaughan Road screaming and waving the bread knife. She
hear somebody screaming loud, loud. At first she didn't
know who it is, and is then she realize that the scream was
coming from she and she couldn't stop it. She dress in she
nightie alone and screaming in the middle of the road. . . .
She wake up the next morning, feeling shaky and something
like spiritual. She was frightened, in case the crying come
back again. . . . She had the feeling that she was holding she
body around she heart, holding sheself together, tight, tight.
She get dressed and went to the Pentecostal Church where she
get married and sit there till evening. For two weeks, this
is all Blossom do. . . . During these weeks, she could drink
nothing but water. (38)

And then, when Blossom taps into the power of the Orisha Oya,
she expresses a sentiment of self-governance and body autonomy—in
essence, she taps into her sacred self. Consider that "Each night Blossom learn a new piece of Oya and finally, it come to she. She had
the power to see and the power to fight; she had the power to feel
pain and the power to heal" (40). Blossom engages in a practice of
self-actualization where she accesses her feelings to determine how
she wants to be a citizen (this does not mean she isn't aware that she
is a citizen in a place where she experiences exclusionary practices
based on identity).

Let's pause for a moment. And in this moment, I encourage
you to journal on the notion of your sacred self—name who you
are. Here are some examples of how Black women have named
themselves:

- "Our relationship to feminism and our world is bound up
  with a proclivity for the percussive, as we divorce ourselves
  from 'correct' or hegemonic ways of being in favor of following the rhythm of our own heartbeats." Crunk Feminist
  Collective
- "I embrace the label of bad feminist because I am human.
  I am messy." (Gay 2014, xi)

As Evans writes, the goal is to recognize "that it is not enough to have my Black and female body sit in a room; I seek to bring my knowledge base to help reshape the relationship of the room, the chair, the table, and how we all think and act as administrators" (12). Once you have named yourself, I think it is a bit easier to determine how to engage the role of chair, as you now have an anchor—a place to rest after meetings where you must remind others that your knowledge is valid. I have used my sacred self to answer the following questions: What do I want to do as chair? How do I want to feel in my role as chair? What are my core values, and how do they influence how I do the work as chair? It is essential to have a strong sense of self in a role that can sometimes feel mundane and thankless. And we come into that sense of self through a practice of naming self.

* * *

Once you have engaged the practice and process of naming yourself, we can begin to think of how this is helpful regarding feelings of citizenship vis-à-vis the department. As I mentioned, I'll focus primarily on interactions with Black men and notions of citizenship. Dawson (2003, 144) writes, "Black women who therefore challenge the black community's patriarchal tendencies are erroneously labeled as race traitors and are accused of being agents of white supremacy (white patriarchy and white feminism)." In your role as chair, some may perceive you as a challenge to the Black male status quo, what I refer to as the Black Maledom. I'm unsure what exactly triggers some Black men to turn on Black women in a particular way. I had a recent experience that made me reflect on Robert Staples's response to Michele Wallace's (1979) *Black Macho and the Myth of the Superwoman* and Ntozoke Shange's (1977) *for colored girls who have considered suicide/when the rainbow is enuf: a choreopoem*. Staples wrote, "I recognize that both women are angry . . . Ms. Wallace gives us the female side and I confess to being troubled at what I hear" (25).

Black Maledom is that sense of male superiority grounded in race, gender, and, in my case, also ethnicity. The Black Maledom in my orbit questioned my leadership when I informed them of what was legal and ethical in a particular case. The response was to question why I was concerned with what was legal, to question my commitment to making a decision that met legal standards. In my role as chair, I had executed my duties; however, I was "cited" as at fault with no reflection on the behaviors of other parties. Eventually, the Black Maledom asserted that I "don't listen!" As with Staples's response to Wallace and Shange, I was construed as "angry." As such, they could justify that they were particularly "troubled" when I asserted that their behaviors met the standard of bullying. Citizenship revoked!

They argued vaguely that I was affected by "something" and had never fully emotionally recovered. I became the incompetent, emotionally unstable individual, while their behaviors were/are left unquestioned, evidence discarded the way that Staples discarded the experiences and evidence of both Wallace and Shange. As I argue in *Shadow Bodies* (2017, 39), in the "racial family," citizenship is not guaranteed for Black women; rather, Black women are used, at times, "to support Black men while marginalizing Black women's issues."

I will not lie to you and tell you that this experience didn't sting. It did. And I found my way through it—by coming back to my identity, my sacred self. Early in my tenure as chair, I crafted my mission and vision statements. My mission statement reads: "To ethically empower others to be their best." This statement allows me to operate from a position of integrity, my landing spot, and an important element for my citizenship of feelings. Before I could craft this mission statement, I engaged in a lot of self-reflection so that what I could actualize was also grounded in integrity. In other words, I had to come to know me and to know me deeply. I was inspired by Black feminists, notably the Combahee River Collective, as I thought of how I wanted to be—to feel and do. In part, *The Combahee River Collective Statement* ([1977] 2015) reads, "As Black feminists and Lesbians we know that we have a very definite revolutionary task to perform, and we are ready for the lifetime of work and struggle before us." I relied on my Black feminist identity to determine what I consider as integrity, which, for me, means recognizing interlocking systems of oppression, self-reflection, and justice. My actions need to flow from this understanding of integrity. And so, my response to the Black Maledom flowed from this point of departure. My revolutionary task involved resistance.

At this point, I invite you to pause and draft your mission statement. Think of the values you hold near and dear to you. Think of how you want to feel in your role as chair and use that to craft your mission statement.

* * *

Finally, let's talk about citizenship of feelings and the institution. Black women leaders in higher education are uncommon. I can quickly count the number of Black women, over twenty years of being in the profession, that I have encountered in administration (this accounts only for the places I worked, and I have worked at a few). According to Whitford (2020), "CUPA-HR's report shows that less than 8 percent of administrators are Black or African American, and more than 80 percent are white." This results, in part, from pipeline issues. Consider that, as reported by the National Center for Education Statistics (2019), "among full-time professors, 53 percent were White males, 27 percent were White females, 8 percent were Asian/Pacific Islander males, and 3 percent were Asian/Pacific Islander females. Black males, Black females, and Hispanic males each accounted for 2 percent of full-time professors."

I won't belabor the point that there is a scarcity of Black women in higher education and that we simply do not make it up through the ranks; thus, there are few of us in administrative roles.

Instead, I want to focus on how some of us navigate the academy, how this impacts how we progress to administration, and how we may engage our administrative roles. In discussing Black professors' departures from the academy, Griffin et al. (2011) write,

> Encounters with racism can be frustrating and hurtful, deterring black scholars from entering academia and leading to early departure from an institution or, more significantly, from academe. . . . Thus, simply examining patterns of institutional departure as an indicator of hostile campus climate may lead to false assumptions about black professors' level of comfort and satisfaction. . . . Rather, departure can be both behavioral

and psychological, ultimately having the potential to affect a
professor's well being in a variety of ways. (497)

Feelings matter. And how we feel as citizens matters. Often, Black
women are ignored, bullied, taxed (with a race-gender tax), isolated,
and the list goes on. As a result, we exit, though not always physi-
cally. Institutions fail to account for multiple types of exiting in their
reporting of retention and attrition rates. But how can institutions
begin to understand Black women's performance in the academy via
a lens of citizenship of feelings in a neo-liberal capitalist structure
that is often divorced from feelings? First, I'm going to tell you that
it is not your role to educate institutions unless there is compensation.
However, you do not have to rest in silence. Audre Lorde tells us
that our feelings can prompt action—liberatory action. Unlike in the
other two instances where I paused and asked you to reflect on your
identity, in this case, I reflect primarily on the identity of institutions.

Institutions first need to recognize how their identities are raced
and gendered. And this does not mean a review of diversity and inclusion statements. It is simply not enough to "welcome" Black women
(and other systematically and institutionally marginalized groups)
to your campus. I would argue that institutions should ban the term
"welcome"—as seen in diversity statements which may talk about a
"welcoming environment." Every time I read such language, I also
read what is not explicitly stated: "and your welcome can be revoked
at any time." It feels trite and liminal. I've seen how my welcome has
expired when I dare to speak of race-gender oppression. Citizenship revoked! So, what is the alternative? Evans writes, "Chairs must
be supported—structurally—to increase opportunities for faculty of
color for promotion, leadership, and retention. Chair stability is campus stability, and we must fundamentally change structures to make
health and wellness possible for chairs of color" (14).

To do this, I recommend that institutions talk to Black women.
Have Black women, and not just those at your institution, design programs and other systems that can address our retention so that we do
not have to perform exits. In thinking of how to ensure full citizenship,
Evans asks, "How might we fundamentally reimagine the department
chair role in a way that creates a new, more socially just normal?" (12).

In the meantime, while we wait for institutions to be responsive to us, we must organize. In my role as chair, I found myself institutionally marginalized for complex reasons. In response, I reached out to several Black-identified women serving as chair and organized a monthly meeting. I'm not suggesting that we do this in lieu of institutional response and accountability, but along with it. We discuss our feelings during our Black women's chair time—what we need to thrive and feel good in our roles. We walk alongside each other, seeing one another when we are often not seen. These women help me to craft my leadership identity.

As I close, I invite you to enter your feeling body as you ponder the following:

1. Who are you as a leader?
2. How do you want to feel in your leadership role?
3. What do you need to be successful in this role?
4. How are you engaging your dean/provost in ensuring that you can be successful?
5. How are you building a community to help you craft your leadership identity?
6. What are you most proud of? Keep that in writing so that you are not twisting in the wind when the winds blow, wondering who you are.

Much love,
Julia S. Jordan-Zachery

References

Brand, Dionne. *Sans Souci and Other Stories*. Ithaca, NY: Firebrand Books, 1989.

Combahee River Collective. *The Combahee River Collective Statement*. United States, 2015. Web Archive. www.loc.gov/item/lcwaN0028151/.

Crunk Feminist Collective. "Mission Statement." *The Crunk Feminist Collective* (blog). crunkfeministcollective.wordpress.com/about/.

Dawson, Michael C. *Black Visions: The Roots of Contemporary African-American Political Ideologies*. Chicago: University of Chicago Press, 2003.

de Brey, Cristobal, Lauren Musu, Joel McFarland, Sidney Wilkinson-Flicker, Melissa Diliberti, Anlan Zhang, Claire Branstetter, and Xiaolei Wang. *Status and Trends in the Education of Racial and Ethnic Groups 2018*. Washington, DC: National Center for Education Statistics, 2019. https://nces.ed.gov/pubsearch/pubsinfo.asp?pubid=2019038.

Evans, Stephanie Y. "Meditations from a Black Woman Chair: Social Justice Values and a New Normal in Academic Administration." *The Department Chair* 32, no. 1 (Summer 2021): 12–15. https://doi.org/10.1002/dch.30395.

Gay, Roxane. *Bad Feminist: Essays*. New York: Harper Perennial, 2014.

Griffin, Kimberly A., Meghan Pifer, Jordan Humphrey, and Ashley Hazelwood. "(Re)Defining Departure: Exploring Black Professors' Experiences with and Responses to Racism and Racial Climate." *American Journal of Education* 117, no. 4 (August 2011): 495–526.

Jones, Tavis A. "A Phenomenological Study of African American Women College and University Presidents: Their Career Paths, Challenges and Barriers." PhD diss., Capella University, 2013. ProQuest (3554921).

Jordan-Zachery, Julia S. "Licking Salt: A Black Woman's Tale of Betrayal, Adversity, and Survival." *Feminist Formations* 31, no. 1 (Spring 2019): 67–84.

———. *Shadow Bodies: Black Women, Ideology, Representation, and Politics*. New Brunswick, NJ: Rutgers University Press, 2017.

Lorde, Audre. *Sister Outsider: Essays and Speeches*. Trumansburg, NY: Crossing Press, 1984.

Marley, Bob. "Exodus." Harry J Studio, 1977.

Monae, Janelle. "I Like That." Warner Chappell Music, Inc., 2018.

Osler, Audrey, and Hugh Starkey. *Changing Citizenship: Democracy and Inclusion in Education*. Berkshire, UK: Open University Press, 2005.

Shange, Ntozake. *for colored girls who have considered suicide/when the rainbow is enuf: a choreopoem*. New York: Macmillan, 1977.

Staples, Robert. "The Myth of Black Macho: A Response to Angry Black Feminists." *The Black Scholar* 10, no. 6/7 (March/April 1979): 24–33.

Wallace, Michele. *Black Macho and the Myth of the Superwoman*. New York: Dial Press, 1979.

Whitford, Emma. "There Are So Few That Have Made Their Way." *Inside Higher Ed*, October 28, 2020. https://www.insidehighered.com/news/2020/10/28/black-administrators-are-too-rare-top-ranks-higher-education-it%E2%80%99s-not-just-pipeline.

6

Dear Dean

*Some Suggestions for Mentoring
Black Women in the Academy*

RÉGINE MICHELLE JEAN-CHARLES
Incoming Director, Northeastern University

Asking the Right Questions

I recently met with a new colleague from Northeastern University, where I now work. He has been here for many years and boasts a treasure trove of knowledge about the university culture and intricate workings. When he contacted me with a request to meet as soon as possible, I was curious about the urgency and wondered what ask he might have for me. Within the first few minutes of our meeting, I was pleasantly surprised. He had one question: "What do you need from me in order for *you* to succeed and reach *your* goals here?" His question caught me off guard. It also flooded my heart with joy. Never before had I encountered someone so explicitly committed to my flourishing. His concern was not about what I could do for the program, or for the institution, but about how my vision would align with my own success.

In all of my years as a professor, such a question had never been posed to me. I have had the privilege of being mentored and well-supported since my years as an undergraduate student and pride myself on being able to identify good mentors. I know well that the best mentors support you in reaching your goals, push you to identify new ones, and do what they can to offer insight and sponsorship along the way.

My new colleague's question was also striking in light of my recent transition from Boston College, where I had been for thirteen years, beginning as an assistant professor and moving through the ranks to become an associate professor with tenure. Much of my decision to move to a new place was due to what I saw as an empowering and refreshing approach to leadership. Considering the conversations with the deans at my now former institution, as well as my current one, a jarring contrast came into focus. One dean, a woman and feminist historian, was keen to glean insights from me. She valued my opinion, requested critical feedback, sought out my thoughts about key projects, and clearly looked at me as a potential thought partner.

Failures of Imagination

Talking with the dean at my former employer, I explained to him what a difference this made to me. I said plainly: "What is most enticing to me about this new position is the dean's commitment to and investment in me as a leader. She has a vision for me as an administrative leader." I then asked: "What is your vision for me?" He paused. "That's a good question . . . that's a really good question . . ." After a long moment he offered, "Well, certainly as a director of African and African Diaspora Studies . . ." His voice trailed off.

I was stunned by his failure of imagination.

What became clear to me in this moment was that the dean did not have a vision for my leadership. He could not see me in any leadership role beyond being a program director. His relegation of me to only African and African Diaspora Studies indicated that he was placing me in the Black box. To be clear, the position of director of Africana Studies is one that I am honored to have. What troubles me, and what the dean exhibited in this moment, was a lack of vision for me beyond program chair. The notion that I would be able to excel as a leader in higher levels of administration had not yet occurred to him.

His view was unexpected and troubling in light of all that I had contributed to the institution over the years. I had been sponsored to participate in the HERS Leadership Institute a few years prior, which should have signaled to him my leadership trajectory.

At an institution with very few pathways into leadership, my constant and consistent engagement should have marked me as someone willing to put herself forward, with a high leadership potential. But it was also a university with a very male-centered and patriarchal structure that was notorious for faring poorly when it came to women's leadership. In fact, when all of the colleges and universities in the state of Massachusetts were ranked in regards to women's leadership, my previous employer was dead last. The study, "Women's Power Gap in Higher Education" (Mach et al. 2019), was the first of its kind to examine leadership trends in higher education in relation to gender as a first step to creating more equitable universities. What this study and others like it confirm is that institutions may claim to value diversity, but fail to take steps to actually share power.

When I decided to leave my position, one of the recurring points nagging at me was the lack of women in leadership roles at the college. Leaving was by no means an easy decision for me, as this was my first academic job, the place where I earned tenure, and where I became who I am as a scholar, teacher, and mentor. When I began as a young mother with a toddler and another child on the way, several women who were senior scholars and administrators offered invaluable mentoring and wisdom that I have tried to pay forward to other women over the years.

In the end, it was the recruiting institution's vision for me as an administrative leader, their commitment to bringing me on as full professor, the dean's intentional mentoring of women faculty and administrators, and the institution's financial commitment to and investment in racial justice that helped me to make the decision in their favor. After the death of George Floyd, my previous institution was one of the many that *for the first time* made public statements decrying racial injustice and professing to take a stance against anti-Black racism and its stain on the United States. What we saw far too often was that this played out as a performance of allyship and solidarity that wasn't as meaningful as it could have been. I was eager to be part of a community where a significant financial commitment to these social justice initiatives was translating into funded action, as well as a more equitably distributed power structure.

Fostering Our Flourishing

Now, having had more time to process my transition and begin in my new role, I write to you in the spirit of improvement with suggestions for how you might better retain Black faculty and foster a better environment for us to flourish in as leaders. This requires funded action and institutional commitment to racial justice rather than the creation of perfunctory task forces that wield little, if any, meaningful power. Allowing Black women faculty to thrive and flourish means being aware of how we will inevitably become tasked (far more than our male colleagues) with diversity and inclusion work, as well as care work for our marginalized students who take comfort in support from faculty who look like them. This emotional labor is exhausting. As many studies have noted, "faculty of color in predominately white institutions experience higher levels of discrimination, cultural taxation, and emotional labor than their white colleagues" (Harris et al. 20).

Following this transition from one institution to another, I have learned to ask different questions of my senior leaders. Rather than consider how I might be of use or service to them, I am now more interested in how they can be of use or service to me. I am interested in how senior leaders can equip and empower me to complete my goals.

Academic Journeys

I began my journey in the academy as an undergraduate student at the University of Pennsylvania. I was attending an intensive one-week summer institute for incoming students, in which we took classes with three professors in different disciplines, and we had the opportunity to take classes with professors in the African American Studies Department. The program exposed us to the wonders and the power of the Black Studies project and served as a gateway for students into the major as well as an introduction to the department. The director of the Mellon Mays Undergraduate Fellowship Program approached me to inquire if I had ever considered becoming a professor. I had not. My plan was to pursue a law degree. As the child of Haitian immigrants, I was raised to believe that I had three options for my future profession: lawyer, medical doctor, or engineer. Since

I was passionate about reading, writing, and talking, I knew that the first option would be the best fit for me. I entered college prepared to pursue a major in politics, philosophy, and economics, which I thought would position me well on the path to becoming an attorney. I knew nothing about people with PhDs other than my assumption that they usually accompanied MDs. Thankfully, the English professor who recruited me into the Mellon Program was able to disabuse me of the notion that law was the only plausible career path for me.

With the help of Mellon, and under the careful mentoring of a Black feminist scholar who took me under her generous wing, I grew in knowledge and insight and chose to study intersections of race and gender in literature. After undergrad, I matriculated into a combined master's and doctoral program at Harvard University, where I wrote a dissertation about representations of gender-based violence in novels by Caribbean and African women writing in French. After spending my final year in Paris at École Normale Supérieure, I graduated from Harvard in six years and then went on to the University of Virginia to be a postdoctoral fellow in the Carter G. Woodson Institute for African and African American Studies. After two years at UVA, I began my first tenure-track position at Boston College, where I went through the ranks from assistant professor to associate professor with tenure. Most recently, I left BC to begin a position at Northeastern University as a full professor and program director. In many ways my professional path was very straightforward. Along the way I have participated in leadership, organizing, and mentoring activities that have re-affirmed my commitment to service, community, and institution building as vital aspects of life in the academy. As I approach the mid-career mark in my journey as a professor, I understand more than ever that, as Lorgia Garcia Peña writes in *Community as Rebellion: A Syllabus for Surviving Academia as a Woman of Color*, "we need to find our people, and together we need to take the resources available to us through our institutions and use them, to build spaces that sustain us" (51).

Black Women Leaders in the Academy Today

When Nikole Hannah-Jones was denied tenure by the board of trustees at the University of North Carolina in 2021, there was some collective head shaking throughout the country. But for Black women in the academy like me, there was head nodding. We had been raised to believe that we had to "work twice as hard" to be considered just as good as our white male peers. We were painfully aware that the academy is far from a meritocracy despite its professed ideals. In fact, the myth of meritocracy was well-documented by Black scholars long before Jones suffered the egregious denial of tenure. Black women faculty and administrators who had a bird's-eye view of how the intersection of race and gender impacts women in higher education were hardly surprised by what happened to Jones. As the authors of *Presumed Incompetent: The Intersections of Race and Class for Women in Academia* make clear, women of color are often misread as being less ambitious and successful. Jones's parting speech acknowledged the unprecedented amount of labor that Black faculty—and women in particular—are called upon to enact in the university, as she declared, "It is not my job to fix what is broken about UNC." At many predominately white institutions, "underrepresented faculty end up devoting intellectual and emotional labor to helping students at a time when they must also produce high-quality research and demonstrate exemplary teaching" (Shayne 2017).

I wholeheartedly agree with the authors of *Stories from the Front of the Room*, who identify recruitment, retention, and recognition as three crucial areas in which administrators can demonstrate their commitment to Black faculty. Because "administrators are the actors who implement the policies of the university that tax faculty of color," much of the burden for how to change this system must rely on them (Harris et al. 98).

When administrators and senior leadership truly embrace equity as a value, rather than deploying it as a buzzword with only symbolic relevance, they will be able to see and recognize us as thought partners and leaders. Recognition matters for at least two reasons. First, it acknowledges and honors faculty of color for the work that we do, and second, it builds an understanding that there is a need for us to be publicly recognized for that work. Coming up with creative ways to reward these faculty for their invisible labor is equally important.

My colleague's question indicated to me that he saw me. He recognized the leadership work I had already done and was expecting me to continue on that trajectory. He showed that he is eager to learn from me, engage me as a thought partner, embrace my vision, and follow me as a leader. Only with true recognition—which involves senior leaders imagining expansive futures for faculty of color, that they then commit to and invest in—can we really thrive.

Sincerely,
Dr. Régine Michelle Jean-Charles

References

Dubé Mach, Christy, Evelyne Murphy, Marta Rosa, and Andrea Silbert. *Women's Power Gap in Higher Education*. Boston: Eos Foundation, 2019.

Garcia Peña, Lorgia. *Community as Rebellion: A Syllabus for Surviving Academia as a Woman of Color*. Chicago: Haymarket Books, 2022.

Gutiérrez y Muhs, Gabrielle, Yolanda Flores Niemann, Carmen G. Gonzalez, and Angela P. Harris, eds. *Presumed Incompetent: The Intersections of Race and Class for Women in Academia*. Salt Lake City: Utah University Press, 2012.

Harris, Michelle, Sherrill Sellers, Orly Clergé, and Frederick W. Gooding, eds. *Stories from the Front of the Room: How Higher Education Faculty of Color Survive & Thrive in the Academy*. New York: Rowman & Littlefield, 2017.

James, Joy, and Ruth Farmer, eds. *Spirit, Space, and Survival: African American Women in (White) Academe*. New York: Routledge, 1993.

Shayne, Julie. "Recognizing Emotional Labor in Academe." *Inside Higher Ed*, September 15, 2017. https://www.insidehighered.com/advice/2017/09/15/importance-recognizing-faculty-their-emotional-support-students-essay.

Stockdill, Brett C., and Mary Yu Danico, eds. *Transforming the Ivory Tower: Challenging Racism, Sexism, and Homophobia in the Academy*. Honolulu: University of Hawaii Press, 2012.

Part II

Letters from Upper Administration

7

How and When I Enter

Pearls of Wisdom for Courageous Leadership in the Academy

CAROL E. HENDERSON

Emory University, Vice Provost for Diversity and Inclusion,
Chief Diversity Officer, Advisor to the President

Dear Incoming Chief Diversity Officer (CDO),

It is such an honor to welcome you into your new role! Congratulations on this achievement. I currently have the privilege of serving in this position, as part of a select group of individuals who have been chosen to lead at such a critical time as this. Chief Diversity Officer roles are proliferating out of need, out of guilt, out of a realization that our country struggles to live up to its own ideals of liberty and justice for all. The truths that we hold self-evident are not self-evident to all. Our communities need you—not only to lead but to speak on behalf of those who have not been afforded the opportunity to enter such a space.

As the inaugural CDO at Emory, I am humbled by the responsibility of such an assignment . . . or should I say a life's mission. I did not arrive at this place on my own. I stand on the shoulders of my grandmother, mother, othermothers, aunties, sisters and sistahs, who thought enough of me to nominate me for leadership positions—to nurture and help cultivate the gifts and talents in me. My responsibility is to fulfill that promise and to help cultivate that promise for others.

That is what the CDO role allows us to do—to champion the intrinsic values of diversity, equity, inclusion, belonging, and justice on behalf of others.* Education is a social justice issue too. And while diversity is not a new thing—humankind has been diverse since the beginning of time—equity and inclusion are the harder virtues to procure. Human nature is anchored in self-preservation, which can cloud our judgment when we think someone is getting preferential treatment or a special pass. It can cause us to be less inclusive in our communities, less willing to set an extra seat at the table, less willing to see the humanity in one another.

Our roles as CDOs require us to advocate for that greater good, to broaden people's perspectives (and our own) on these very topics. As thought leaders, we must model collaboration. As accountability partners, we must stretch our communities to have those prickly discussions about the legacies of racism, inhumaneness, bias, and discrimination, in order to accelerate our institutions' movement toward restorative justice. It is in this space that we work collectively and diligently to address and name those inequities. This is where we remind each other that education is about opportunity, and is one of the few pathways in our society that facilitates social mobility.

As a first-generation student and a former mother on AFDC,† education was my saving grace. It allowed me to shift the economic trajectory of my immediate family. It enabled me to educate my son. But education also has the ability to ensnare. Student loan debt is real, and many students and their families have traded in the ability to own a home for educating their children. Some students mortgage their very futures to experience the community higher education provides. And as a Black woman, I know—like many of us do—that all educational experiences are not equal. It is commonly known that the academy was not created for us. Nor is the academy willing to make seismic shifts to welcome all to its hallowed halls. It

---

* For a description of the chief diversity officer role, please see "What Is a Chief Diversity Officer: Higher Education Perspective," Damon A. Williams and Katrina Wade-Golden, *Diversity Officer Magazine* (2018).

† AFDC stands for Aid for Families with Dependent Children, a public assistance program established in 1935.

can be unyielding in its insistence on relegating us to its margins—in the classroom, in the curriculum, in the legislative halls of decision-making. But we must claim our seat at the table. As Shirley Chisholm reminds us, if they don't give you a seat at the table, bring your own chair.

We must ALWAYS have hope. I refuse to relinquish that—and I hope you will hold hope close to your heart, let it saturate your very being. You come from a long line of educational leaders who had enough hope to create the path for us to arrive at this space and time. Mary McLeod Bethune. Anna Julia Cooper. Fanny Jackson Coppin. Ruth Simmons. Johnnetta Cole. Leaders in higher education have an obligation to maintain an equity-minded lens in this work—to be conscious of the historical obstacles that constrict access to higher education, academically and materially. Equity-mindedness calls for us to take personal and institutional responsibility for eliminating barriers, for identifying patterns of inequality that perpetuate themselves in admissions processes, curricula development, classroom experiences, and scholarly evaluation. Although student scholars are the heartbeat of our educational institutions, our work in equity-mindedness must extend to those who teach, create, innovate, and mentor—our faculty—and to those whose dedications and talents sustain the operational efficiency and effectiveness of our institutions, our staff.

Having spent over two decades in the classroom at the University of Delaware, and over twenty-six years in higher education, twelve of those years in various leadership positions as a chair, vice provost, and community leader, I've seen how the ecosystem of higher education demands that we be in tune with all of the operational components of an institution as CDO practitioners. "Leaks in the pipeline" can occur at any point in the process. Pathways to the process are full of broken dreams, broken promises, and sadly, broken souls. Please know that I am not saying it's our charge alone to repair the leaks. Many of us as CDOs are trying to keep ourselves from going down the drain—tired, disillusioned, bitter, exhausted (did I say tired??)—because we couldn't do more. As the visionaries for a better day, we have to be careful to guard our minds, our hearts, and our spirits—we must hold on to the essence of our integrity as human beings.

People are looking to us to lead, not manage the work of DEI. Managing is transactional. It *can* be perfunctory. Leading is transformational. It is the work of thought leadership. It is intentional. Leadership taps into your ability to influence and motivate others to contribute to the success of the institution, to inspire others to stretch into a more equitable and inclusive future. Inspiring hope does not mean we have all the answers as CDOs. Nor does it mean that we ignore the realities of our work. There will be people who don't agree with the intention of this work—who will be downright hostile to the ideas of representational diversity, inclusion, and equity. That is to be expected. We are not all the same, and some people are just toxic and mean, angry at the world and the fact that you are in it. In *productive* conversations, these engagements can stretch us in our leadership roles. They may require us to innovate, be creative, and cultivate a different kind of accountability. I've found that I do not have to dictate, micromanage, stifle, or control the soul of the work. Just provide room for it to breathe.

And breathe is an apt metaphor for the work that must be done in this era. A cataclysmic 2020 saw a global pandemic take the lives of more than 5 million people worldwide, over 750,000 in the United States alone. This disease is still taking lives, exacerbating the inequities of our society in glaring and undeniable ways. Many institutions having to shift to remote education meant shoring up—or creating—an infrastructure that afforded students a better chance for success. Early studies show that we have not gotten this right, nor have we seen the full contours of the impact of COVID-19 on higher education. Generational wealth will shift as loss of family income, jobs, and businesses widens further the divide between the haves and the have nots. Add to this the racial fatigue, angst, and spiritual woundedness of Black and Brown people forced to witness and absorb the murders of George Floyd, Breonna Taylor, Ahmaud Arbery, Rayshard Brooks, and countless others, and you realize how important your voice is at this crucial moment.

But it is also important for you to know your lane. It is critical for you to know the context you have to operate in—to be conscious. I have found a number of our colleagues being plugged into gaps in neglected areas in the operations of institutions too large to fill. They do not have the institutional support, institutional resources, or institutional authority to enact change. Yet they are fearless, resilient, and committed to the work. They realize that change, although slow, is constant. They want to capitalize on the energy of the social activism that has brought us to this current precipice where there is an opportunity for real change—beyond institutional statements, beyond the rhetoric of the obvious. You can help to lead transformation that has at its core an accountability rooted in the educational mission and vision of the institution. This collaborative work acknowledges the unheralded work of the forerunners who paved the way. They may not have been the inaugural CDO or the vice provost, but they championed equity, diversity, inclusion, and justice, nonetheless. I provide room here to thank them for paving that way.

As you consider the journey ahead—and the many communities you must attend to—I would like to share some uncommon pearls of wisdom that I hope will guide you on your sojourn. I call them uncommon because these pearls—priceless in value—were forged through struggle, resilience, fortitude, and a gracious pressure that gives rise to excellence. Pearls symbolize wisdom gained through experience. They are an emblem of integrity. As a leader, people have to trust you. That trust is earned through the integrity of your work. Your dedication and results-driven outcomes will be the way you build a bridge to a community who is depending on you to act.

These signposts—I call them "the beatitudes of leading for impact"—have self and community at their core. **You can't lead if you don't take care of yourself.** You will have no wellspring to draw your inspiration from if your own repository is spiritually, emotionally, and intellectually depleted. Those of us who fly are always cautioned to put our own oxygen masks on before helping others in the event of a loss of cabin pressure. In our roles as CDOs, we should follow the same principles in the event of an institutional crisis. We may experience a loss of cabin pressure in the organization as a result of many things—the mass exodus of HUGs* faculty or staff in a college or unit; an accessibility service disconnect that not only affects student academic performance but exacerbates an already fragile campus

---

* HUGs are defined as historically underrepresented and underserved groups for this discussion.

climate; a racialized incident that traumatizes and triggers communities on and off campus. Any of these "cabin pressure" moments will ask you to center your leadership in what I call **leadership GRIT: Grace, Resilience, Intuitive Intellectual Capacity, and Tonality.**[*]

Grace entails forgiving yourself and others. The work of diversity, equity, and inclusion requires grace. Progress in DEI will require grace as well. I had someone recently ask me to define grace as it relates to leadership. Grace is what it is—giving people something they have not earned, and in some cases, do not deserve. All of us fall into these categories at some time in our professional and personal lives. If the common good is your objective, then grace is a transformative tool to allow people to reorient themselves, to forgive themselves as they take this journey to a more equitable and inclusive community. You will need to extend this same privilege to yourself, as leadership is not about perfection. It is about setting a course, developing a blueprint to commence that journey, only to understand that, as blueprints indicate, there will be changes. Being nimble is one of the other skills we must have as leaders. And it will take your fortitude—your **resilience** as an advocate and change agent—to guide the community into and through the impending crisis. Your intuition, your experience having journeyed through difficult terrain in the academy before is a treasure trove you must draw from, in order to hear and attend to the needs of your community. Mindful listening goes a long way when chaos is in the room. Being heard is one of the greatest gifts we can bequeath to each other. It recenters our focus in that moment and reorients us to the humanity in each other.

Remember why you took the journey in the first place. Do your Soul work. Soul work is defined as work that keeps you grounded in your authentic self. It is also that work that lets you know you are a part of something larger than yourself. It is about legacy and responsibility. I am on this journey because someone paved the way for me, passed me the mantle, and now I pass that mantle to you. And it is about more than just accepting a position. I feel humbled to

---

[*] My Leadership GRIT paradigm is influenced by the excellent work of Angela Duckworth, Williams James, K.E. Ericson, Malcolm Gladwell, and so many others. I want to acknowledge that here.

have been chosen to lead. I know that the challenges of leading can make you question why you decided to assume a leadership role in the first place. But my god mom told me once, when I was hesitant about assuming the responsibility of a new leadership role, that I was not given the talents and gifts I have to sit on them. Keep them dormant. She said there was a community waiting for me to share in the journey of change. And that my experiences meant I would contribute something meaningful to the conversation that only I could add. Even in this arena, where DEI is the anchor for many a conversation, there is always room to do more work, to create more pathways to intentional and transformational possibilities. Embrace that. Leverage your growth mindset to nourish your passion and purpose.

Create legacy goals. When I joined the Emory community in 2019, one of the things then Provost Dwight McBride asked his executive leadership team was what our legacy goals were. It was a wonderful query, one that has impacted how I approach my work in DEI. Our intentional work—if it is intentional—must be sustained in an infrastructure that outlives our time in our role. These goals are aspirational as we develop the building blocks of transformation to achieve them.

Never stop learning. Is there more I need to say here? A dormant mind is a stagnant one. We should be lifelong learners. Individuals who reach for more knowledge to inspire others to do the same. Much is gained in the process of learning as a leader. One of the most important things you learn is that you are human. You will misstep. You will have small victories as well. In each experience is the lesson. And hopefully that lesson will lead you closer to your hoped-for goal.

As I reflect on this letter that I am writing, I am inspired by the promise that lies ahead for you. I hope you will consider developing your own uncommon pearls of wisdom—fashioned from your own sojourn as a transformative leader in our community. In sharing our wisdom, we give others permission *to be*. That is the most valuable gift we can give to ourselves and others as we recommit daily to creating that beloved community where all are welcomed.

May your gifts make room for you in the journey ahead.

In gratitude,
Carol

References

Brown, Elaine M., Marsha Haygood, and Rhonda J. McLean. *The Little Black Book of Success: Laws of Leadership for Black Women*. London: One World Publishers, 2010.

Duckworth, Angela. *GRIT: The Power of Passion and Perseverance*. New York: Scribner, 2018.

Evans, Stephanie Y. *Black Women in the Ivory Tower, 1850–1954: An Intellectual History*. Gainesville: University Press of Florida, 2008.

Harts, Minda. *The Memo: What Women of Color Need to Know to Secure a Seat at the Table*. New York: Hachette Book Group, Inc., 2019.

Hodges, Carolyn R., and Olga M. Welch. *Truth Without Tears: African American Women Deans Share Lessons in Leadership*. Cambridge, MA: Harvard Education Press, 2018.

Williams, Damon A., and Katrina C. Wade-Golden. "What Is a Chief Diversity Officer?: A Higher Education Perspective." *Diversity Officer Magazine*, 2018. Accessed November 7, 2021. https://diversityofficermagazine.com/leadership/what-is-a-chief-diversity-officer-higher-education-perspective/.

Williams, Pat, and Jim Denney. *The Leadership Excellence Devotional*. Uhrichsville, OH: Barbour Publishing, Inc., 2013.

Worthington, Roger L., Christine A. Stanley, and Daryl G. Smith. *Standards of Professional Practice for Chief Diversity Officers in Higher Education, 2.0*. Fort Lauderdale, FL: National Association of Diversity Officers in Higher Education, 2020. https://nadohe.memberclicks.net/standards-of-professional-practice-for-chief-diversity-officers.

8

Lift as We Climb and When We Get There, Mentor Others

THERESA RAJACK-TALLEY
Vice Provost for Equity and Inclusion,
Dalhousie University, Nova Scotia, Canada

Dear Black and Racialized Female Senior Administrators,

We start our chapters with a reflection on our life journeys because as Black and racialized* women, we cannot separate our lived selves and intellectualism from our professional and administrative roles, *and we should not.* Our personal and professional experiences inform and reify each other in very positive ways. As such, my modus operandi as a racialized female administrator is greatly influenced by my lived experiences. In this chapter, I have been asked to reflect on my journeys, share some lessons learned along the way, and suggest ways in which others on similar paths can navigate for success the many complexities, and nuanced and difficult challenges.

---

* Racialization refers to a system of social stratification that occurs through the promulgation of overt and covert ideologies of racial difference and privilege (see chapter one in *Living Racism* by C. Talley, 2018)

Reflections on My Journey

THE PASSAGE

Some people are positioned to choose their own career path, but for others, life's journey chooses our career trajectory. Growing up as a child in a small rural village in the Caribbean, social class differences were visible all around me, manifested in disparities in material wealth and social capital, both important to educational attainment and life chances. The kids in my elementary school and village were of the same racial/ethnic heritage and so the concept of racialization was not obvious. But, from this youthful age, I detected in myself an awareness that life experiences would lead me down a career path filled with briars of injustices. My commitment, understanding, and social justice actions grew wider and stronger through my secondary education, undergraduate, and graduate programs, where I was exposed to racial inequality and other social inequities. Like so many other Black and racialized women, my exposure to human rights issues—including systemic racism, sexism, and their intersectionality—influenced my professional career and *unapologetically so*.

Over the life of my profession, my social activism expanded to become more inclusive of the many forms of discrimination and oppression arising from emergent multiplicity and intersectionality of identities. My diplomas, research, teaching, service, and administrative positions remained tied to social justice issues across diaspora boundaries and stretched over four different universities in three countries. My original home in Trinidad and Tobago continues to grapple with its social stratification including the racial/ethnic dynamics of two major diasporas—African and East Indian—along with gender identities and social class hierarchies arising from a history of colonialism, slavery, and indentureship. This is not to discount the pressures of continued Eurocentrism and North American influence on all fronts.* While race relations in North America are different from the Caribbean, I was quickly sensitized through a social

---

* For historical social analyses, see Oliver C. Cox (1948), "Caste, Class & Race: A Study in Social Dynamic."

justice lens, educational pursuits, and the life and people I choose to live and work with in the US.

Twenty years in a Black Studies Department in Louisville, Kentucky, and married to an African American who was a race scholar, social activist, and mentor, taught me how to critically analyze this environment, survive, and succeed. I moved from assistant to full professor in Pan-African Studies and served as a vice chair, as well as director of graduate programs in the department for over a decade. Later I became the chair and subsequently an associate dean in the College of Arts and Sciences for International Programs, Diversity, and Community Engagement, focused on the African American community. This journey involved navigating systemic racism, sexism, classism, and the other forms of social stratification of the North American mosaic and its academies. The lessons learned and experiences gained in the US are transferable skills that I took with me to my current position as a vice provost in another university and country. Before leaving my previous position, I tried to make sustainable the social transformation programs that I had invested much of my time in—through mentoring others (as I was also mentored) to be successful—to continue to build, expand, and enhance programs aimed at addressing social inequities.

COLONIALISM EVERYWHERE

Since colonialism and social justice issues including racism, sexism, homophobia, social class, and cultural discrimination (and their various permutations) are global, when my life journey transported me to another land and space, I experienced both similar and new social inequities. Now in Canada at Dalhousie University in Halifax, I had to learn about the colonial histories and outcomes of the Indigenous and Black communities of the region. The African Nova Scotians, who are the most long-standing Black communities in Canada, and the Indigenous peoples of Canada (First Nations, Inuit, and Metis) have been racialized, disenfranchised, and discriminated against for centuries. Dalhousie University is located in Mi'kma'ki, the ancestral and unceded territory of the Mi'kmaq, who have been here for thousands of years. One of the key lessons that I had to quickly ascertain when working with the two groups is their core philosophy and modus operandi of "nothing about us without us."

My original goal was never to seek senior leadership positions in the academy because of the many stresses of managing personalities and politics, as well as the limitation of having to represent an institution founded on colonialism and at the same time work to transform the institution. I wanted to avoid the difficulties of being responsible for addressing deep-seated, wide-ranging issues of diversity, equity, inclusiveness, and accessibility. And then, there are the inherent challenges of having a racialized, gendered, and immigrant identity in a space where, as Canadian scholar-administrator Malinda Smith explains, "when I walk into a room, [I] look around me and I'm the only non-white person there."* But for Black and racialized women like myself, there is always that "itch" called social obligation that causes us to want to scratch away at patriarchy and Eurocentrism whenever the opportunity behooves us.

Unfortunately, even as senior administrators, our voices can be muffled, and we are sometimes psychologically (for fear of being stereotyped) and/or economically (from a need for job security) bullied into silence and/or accommodation. I see the peer-mentoring network of Chair at the Table, a research collective established in the spring of 2018, as a powerful social movement that has broken the unsettling silence of Black women leaders in the academy and is redefining leadership from Black women's standpoint and intellect. We openly share ideas, knowledge, experiences, challenges, and recommendations in safe spaces. The scholarly publications of this social movement are creative, informative, and challenging to the dominant white patriarchal administrators and discriminatory practices in the academy. The Chair at the Table social movement gives me confidence that we can mentor and be mentored, and through this process change the academy.

---

* As quoted in Harriet Eisenkraft, "Racism in the academy."

Scope, Challenges, and Lessons Learned as a Vice Provost

THE SCOPE AND RESPONSIBILITIES

The provost is the chief executive officer for the administration of the university. Vice provosts support the provost by providing leadership in all areas of academic policies, programs, and personnel. Core to my position as the Vice Provost for Equity and Inclusion (VPEI) is advising the president, provost, deans, and other senior leadership on all matters related to equity, diversity, inclusion, and accessibility (EDIA), both on and off campus. Fundamental to the role is addressing systemic racism, sexism, homophobia, anti-Semitism, Islamophobia, and other forms of discrimination through the Human Rights and Equity Services, strategic planning, policy and practices, research and education, and cultural shifts. Years of experience and understanding of the structural/systemic "isms" of the academy have taught me that achieving any level of equity success requires the creation, expansion, and enhancement of spaces that empower marginalized, racialized, and underrepresented voices. It requires building on the work of so many that came before to break barriers. And it involves joining forces with those who are still here advocating for all aspects of equity and inclusiveness that are imperative to decolonizing the academic empire.

Successful transformation requires sustainability that goes beyond special projects, programs, or a few personnel. As the Vice Provost for Equity and Inclusion, it is important to provide leadership in building EDIA decision-making structures and processes across campus and to embed these in the university's functionality similar to how Wi-Fi technology is now central to the operations of the university. This can be achieved and sustained through university-wide committees and not just one diversity officer or advisory group. It requires capacity building in the following areas: (1) recruitment and retention of diverse faculty, staff, and senior and mid-level leaders; (2) a commitment to underrepresented student access and success, with a focus on students from local and/or Indigenous communities; (3) diversity and inclusiveness in curriculum, teaching design, and pedagogies; (4) diversity excellence in research and innovation; (5) a culture of inclusiveness around differences (rather than hierarchical or forced assimilation) for a healthy and safe campus climate; and (6) partnerships with communities to remain grounded as a civic university.

Lastly, it necessitates challenging and, where appropriate, changing the criterion we inherited and defend as academic integrity without admitting that these metrics were created to maintain the exclusion and oppression of diverse populations. Of course, there are many challenges in trying to meet these inspirational and aspirational goals. Below I highlight a few key operational barriers and discuss some strategies used to successfully overcome some of them.

STRATEGIES FOR NAVIGATING PRACTICAL CHALLENGES

It is quite common that diversity officer positions in universities and colleges, including at senior leadership levels, are filled by capable and qualified Black and other racialized women. It is also common that diversity and equity positions (and others) that we occupy are undervalued and can be perceived as tokenistic, with similar negative stereotypes toward both you and the job that people associate with affirmative action. With little to no resources but with many expectations of the position, oftentimes it can feel as if we are being set up to fail (intentionally or unintentionally). This is not surprising, as I explain in a piece published in *Palimpsest: A Journal on Women, Gender, and the Black International*, entitled "We Do Not Have to Be White or Men to Lead: Redefining and Assessing Black Women's Leadership." Black women are on the one hand exceptionalized as Black matriarchal superwomen or superhumans who could do what men cannot, and on the other hand, viewed as not as strong as male leaders, but merely as "fixers," with some level of organizing skills. Butch Lee (2015) points out that the tendency of white patriarchy to exceptionalize and trivialize at the same time is steeped in the historical interpretation of Harriet Tubman as simply "helping others." Tubman is cast in "the maternal role of nurturer," rather than as a "combatant, a guerrilla, a warrior," a true freedom fighter in the anti-slavery underground and, I would add, as an intellect.

We are still seen as this prototype in contemporary times. We are rarely offered opportunities or resources as we are not recognized as capable leaders; instead, these spaces are protected for privileged whites and/or males. If we do get one of the few high-level administrative leadership positions available, it is important to assess whether the resources needed to achieve the overwhelming goals set upon us are provided. If not, as is often the case, we can become frustrated, experience physical and mental health distress, or in a worst-case scenario—fail. To navigate this situation requires resourcefulness, creativity, drawing on our diverse experiences and broad multifunctional leadership skills, and, most importantly, relying on our *intellect and critical analysis skills*, qualities usually not associated with us. Below, I offer four strategies that I adopted.

The first strategic step is to do an informal rapid institutional analysis of the university and discover where the resources important to your work are located. Universities do possess wide-ranging resources, although getting this type of support requires spending a fair amount of time and human interactions on building relationships, earning respect, and educating others on the needs and benefits of the work. Particularly important to getting support for EDIA goals and projects is to provide evidence-based arguments through relevant disaggregated data that shows inequities based on race, ethnicity, gender identity, and other social indicators and their intersectionality.

A second strategy I gathered from understanding the histories of Black Studies, Women and Gender Studies, and Queer Studies. These educational programs were born out of social movements to fill academic needs. Strategically aligning yourself and the work of your office with current social justice issues and movements, and collaborating with the campus caucuses and other socially conscious elements, helps in advocating for resources and actions. For example, you could work with members of the Black Faculty and Staff Caucus or other groups to create Black Studies and Black Studies Research Institutes, levying this work as part of an institutional response to the Black Lives Matter (BLM) movement and to the academy's racist, sexist, and colonial history. In Canada we also draw on the educational and research recommendations found in the "Truth &

Reconciliation Commission of Canada: Calls for Action Report" to garner support for Indigenous groups on campus.[*]

Third, linking the university's EDIA core values with institutions nationally is also a useful strategic tactic. As a senior administrator, you can provide leadership for the university's endorsements and support for current social justice initiatives in the academy. For example, I volunteered to serve on the organizing committee for a National Dialogue on Anti-Black Racism, ensuring that many from the university participated and followed up in crafting and soliciting institutional endorsements of a National Charter on Anti-Black Racism and Black Inclusion in universities and colleges.[†] This type of work is important in increasing the number of advocates working to achieve EDIA goals within the walls of the academy, securing institutional commitments, and helping to develop a national agenda.

Further, communicating the university's EDIA mission and your work to the public is critical in soliciting support, awareness, security, accountability, and in educating the wider off-campus community. Present and participate in public forums as a representative of senior leadership with a Black or racialized female perspective. Additionally, create your own public forum, one that allows marginalized and/or underrepresented voices to speak about social justice issues from their standpoints. Together with three women volunteer staffers, we started *The Speak Truth to Power* forum, which was born out of the pain of the George Floyd justice movement, but soon expanded to address all forms of racism, discrimination, and oppression. The forum is designed so those most affected can speak the truth from their perspectives and educate anyone willing to learn. The forum partners with underrepresented communities, hoping to enact change or, at a minimum, instill greater understanding, compassion, and knowledge. Recordings of events are used as educational tools and have become strategically important to the work, as it is now public and reflective of the institution's commitment to EDIA.

---

[*] https://ehprnh2mwo3.exactdn.com/wp-content/uploads/2021/01/Calls_to_Action_English2.pdf

[†] www.utsc.utoronto.ca/principal/scarborough-charter

These are just a few operational and practical strategies that have worked successfully at my institution, as we try to navigate difficulties for Black and racialized women at all levels and ranks in the academy. As part of the Chair at the Table mentorship effort, I have analyzed and discussed *one* of the many challenging phenomena—the role of white women in academia—that is commonly experienced but rarely brought out into the open.

White Women Allies?

There is still a demographic asymmetry of white male leaders in the academy—from presidents and vice presidents to provosts and vice provosts, to chairs and deans. The old boy network is old news but a persistent powerhouse. It is still customary practice for men to make decisions about us and for us. What is less admonished but also a powerful force that has an impact upon Black and racialized women's (and men's) experiences in the academy is the role of white women. In many North American universities and colleges, white women fall below white men in tenured, full professorships and administrative positions, but they do comprise approximately half of all employees. They are not a homogenous group, certainly. Historically, *some* white women were abolitionists, while others owned slaves in the American South and stood to "personally and directly benefit from their commodification . . . they were not all bystanders, but co-conspirators" (Jones-Rodgers 2019, 205). Today, race continues to play a role *within* gender, impacting the distribution of social and material capital in the academy, as well as causing psychological effects across populations.

To understand persistent racial etiquette[*] within gender, I use two relevant rules of the Jim Crow Guide cited in Talley and Rajack-Talley (2018). One stipulates that a Black (or racialized person) never asserts or even intimates that a white person may be lying (or performing

---

[*] Racial etiquette is the term used to describe how the social relations between persons bounded by hierarchical racial classifications manifest in private and public spheres. It is observed through racial practices, traditions, and customs, and reflects the racial beliefs of individuals and groups (see Talley and Rajack-Talley 2018).

inefficiently). A more contemporary explanation-expansion of this rule appears in Ruby Hamad's 2020 book, *White Tears/Brown Scars: How White Feminism Betrays Women of Color*. Like Hamad and many of you, I too have heard about/encountered incidents where white women's race and gender have been leveraged in ways that harm Black and racialized women in the academy. There is a tendency to ignore, excuse, or explain away reports by Black and racialized women of their experiences of racism by white women. This is the result of years of normalization of gendered racialization that perpetuates stereotypes from a white privileged lens, through which Black and racialized women are seen as strong matriarchs and white women as *distressed damsels*!

Many Black and racialized women, particularly staff who are the most vulnerable, for decades quietly survive toxic work environments, and in some cases reach mental health breaking points. I have become quite sensitive to the workings of gendered white privilege that has normalized disparities in women's access to resources and opportunities for promotion and, worse yet, penalizes and causes harm to Black and racialized women (and men). We should pay attention to Frances Ellen Watkins Walker's warnings that white women navigate existing systems to gain advantages, which sometimes means manipulating and dominating women of color and adopting the archetype of the damsel in distress (cited in Hamad 2020, 93–97).

The second Jim Crow rule that seems to be in effect in these situations suggests that we should never lay claim to, or overtly demonstrate, superior knowledge or intelligence over whites. While this pertains to any field, it is most evident when white women (and men) are pressed to let us know that they know more about our lived experiences and our work than we do. Even at a senior administrator level, there are instances where your expertise, intellect, and managerial abilities are challenged, and you are advised to consult with someone else (most likely white), who is believed to be more proficient, and/or decisions are made for you under the aegis of being "*in your best interest*."

Not only are we judged differently and more harshly but we are constantly under a microscope, where if we err (real or perceived), white women tattle and portray us as ineffective leaders. They may sometimes receive (unintentional or intentional) material and social capital from the white males with whom they share information, who buy into the white damsel in distress concept, and who are often more comfortable with white young women than with Black women (and Black males) of any age. As a racialized female administrator, I challenge and am challenged in addressing inequities within gender as much as across race and other identities.

Compared to Black and racialized women, white women predominate at all levels of the academy as supervisors, managers, faculty members, staff, and some senior leaders. They have benefited over the years by accumulating opportunities, experience, and knowledge on the operations of the academy, and garnering some decision-making powers. Not all are adversaries, as some are willing collaborators in ways critical to transforming the institution, including increasing access to resources for Black, other racialized, and/or under-represented groups in the academy. The lesson learned is to take the time to discover who are genuine allies based on their actions rather than make assumptions based on rhetoric.

Allyship can only be established when white women (and men) recognize their own biases (comforts) and privileges, and how their actions and racial etiquette practices described above have an impact on Blacks and racialized others. This includes acknowledging the disparities in how opportunities and resources are allocated, as well as the biased and unfair evaluations and judgments of performance based on race, gender, and other social variables. But also, as Hamad points out, it is important to understand how white "tears" (and white male voices) are treated, versus how Black and racialized women are treated when they report their stressful experiences. Too often, when incidents of racial bias or racism are raised, Black and other racialized individuals are made to feel like confronters, while white female perpetrators present themselves as victims who are wrong-fully accused. Whether the bias is conscious or unconscious, the negative and usually painful outcome is the same for Blacks and racialized individuals. Further, if certain actions directed at a Black or racialized individual are seen as "unintentional," these same actions are often not viewed as "intentional" when directed toward a white person. But as women who have walked this path filled with briars of injustice—and who are still here—we can share hope, strategies, and lessons learned with each other.

My Top Recommendations

Seek, apply, bridge, and create. Many of us lack confidence, not so much in ourselves but in the possibility of getting certain positions. Nevertheless, you should apply for any type/level of administrative opportunity if you so desire. You may have to purposively seek out these opportunities, as they are usually not widely known to us because we are excluded from those information networks. Consequently, the few of us who are administrators should consciously reach out, facilitate, and build bridges for underrepresented members to get the experience and qualifications they need for administrative opportunities. Lift as we climb, and when we get there, mentor others to make the climb. Additionally, we need to be courageous and create *new opportunities* for administrative experiences specific to Black and racialized women (and men). Be confident and advocate: let the academy know (loudly) that Black and racialized women (and men) do not get the opportunities that whites get—the acting positions, directors, the vice-chair-dean-provost spots, etc. Real change means that we must break the "mini-me" white syndrome. We must educate the organization, especially senior leadership, on the urgency, need, nature, time, and resources required for such complex changes, as well as the many benefits gained through diversification, inclusiveness, and equity.

Build the right types of allyship. It is guaranteed that we will experience micro and macro aggressions and sometimes be accused of them ourselves. Be prepared, assess points and levels of resistance, and acknowledge and manage conflict early in the role. Resistance and aggression are expected from white privileged groups. Allyship with whites in the academy can only be built with those who are committed to learning (not telling us) about the barriers we experience, who understand, and who are willing to use their own privileges in the interest of others. Expect that there are also conflicts within and amongst diverse groups that require navigation and a different approach. As the most visible agent of change, we are also the moving target for all those who are afraid and/or who do not trust us. One of the most eye-opening lessons I learned as an administrator is that while you think people are interacting with you because of who you are, oftentimes they respond and judge you based on who they are.

The safest way of addressing the multiplicity of diverse identities and issues is to build a coalition of allies by first recognizing and then working across differences. Coalition and allyship are important in navigating known (and some unknown) barriers and within the premise that equity is not a zero-sum game. It is about being cautious of not falling into the trap of *crabs in a barrel*, climbing on each other for resources and opportunities, rather than working together for the allocation of what is required to meet common as well as specific gaps and needs. Good allyship is core to developing effective strategies to combat systemic issues.

Promote transparency and community engagement. I am a firm believer in a participatory modus operandi, which I assess to be a characteristic of Black women's style of leadership (see Rajack-Talley 2021). Collaborating with the Indigenous community here, I also learned the difference between consultation, which is very Eurocentric and disempowering, and engagement, which is more about partnership and respect. Integral to this type of administration is communicating frequently and effectively your ideas and work at the intellectual and emotional levels, and doing so to everyone—all stakeholders—students, faculty, staff, campus groups, and the community. The higher you move in administration, the greater the perception and expectation that your allegiance is with senior administration, and with an institution often associated with colonial traditions of white privilege and patriarchy. To counteract these beliefs, establish and/or maintain a close alliance with various caucuses, racial/ethnic/gendered members of the academy, and the wider marginalized community off campus. These relationships keep you grounded and real, so you never lose sight of the prize/cause. They provide support and a level of security for the challenging/unpopular perspectives and decisions that you will have to make or advocate for that do not conform to the traditions of the academy.

Seek mentorship. In administration, it is more difficult to find mentors at the same level who look like you or me, so you may have to seek such mentors off campus. I have found great Black female (and male) mentors who may have had linkages with the academy, or are independent of the academy and well accomplished in their own right. I also seek refuge, comfort, and advice from the narratives, histories, activism, and intellectual traditions of Black women's voices in books and articles (see the Black Women's Studies Booklist: bwstbooklist.net). Even as I write this chapter navigating the contention and conflict of EDIA issues, I found myself reading the biography of Harriet Tubman. As Black and racialized women administrators, we work through the complexities produced by the intersection of our race *and* gender as well as *within* race and gender. As Bay et al. (2015) explain in *Toward an Intellectual History of Black Women*, "Black women thinkers move through space, time and many spheres of ideas and actions" (5). My own lived and professional journeys are evidence of this.

Some Concluding Thoughts

In the first iteration of this article, I had not written a conclusion, because I could not conceptualize an end to my journey for social justice and human rights. It takes many years of tiresome navigation to get to any level of academic administration. I borrow from Fannie Lou Hamer's speech, delivered with Malcolm X at a rally at the Williams Institutional CME Church, Harlem, New York, in 1964, "*I've been tired so long, now I am sick and tired of being sick and tired.*"* When I get to this point, and so too will you, I recall what two of my Black male social justice warriors and mentors, Jan Carew and Clarence Talley, advised. That it is okay to give yourself time to be sad and angry, but Jan said, "*Take thirty minutes for this and then move on,*" and Clarence reminded me, "*There is too much work to be done to get consumed with anger, frustration, and sadness.*" The experience of a university administrator with a social justice commitment to fighting the impact of institutional colonization also involves managing the frustrating and difficult behavior of individuals of all identities.

---

* https://awpc.cattcenter.iastate.edu/2019/08/09/im-sick-and-tired-of-being -sick-and-tired-dec-20-1964/

Clarence warned not to expend a lot of brain energy on such individuals, "*unless you want to be like them. You should concern yourself only with what you are comfortable doing and being.*"

Dear Black and racialized women, you all have experienced and/or witnessed some of the difficulties in climbing the academic ladder, but do not be afraid. If you are reading this chapter and this book, this suggests that you are already on this journey (or at least thinking about it). You/we are all natural rebels, a term Hilary Beckles (1989) used to describe enslaved women who regularly resisted slavery and never accommodated the system, but fought in any way that they could. For my co-authors and others, I quote Albert "Nuh" Washington (2002), who explains that "*in struggling you never lose . . . ideas live within people . . . and so it is incumbent upon us to teach others . . . to leave our legacy on a higher level. . . . victory is the knowledge that others will carry on, and as long as that is going on there is no defeat.*" We understand that universities and colleges were never built for us or about us and only we as a collective can change them. To all, believe in yourself, believe in the collective, and seek us out. You are not alone. Stay safe, be well, and pause when needed. Thanks for allowing me to share myself. And although I am sick and tired of being sick and tired, you will always have my support.

—*Theresa Ann*

References

Bay, Mia, Farah J. Griffin, Martha S. Jones, and Barbara D. Savage. *Toward an Intellectual History of Black Women*. Chapel Hill: University of North Carolina Press, 2015.

Beckles, Hilary McD. *Natural Rebels: A Social History of Enslaved Black Women in Barbados*. New Brunswick, NJ: Rutgers University Press, 1989.

Cox, Oliver C. *Caste, Class & Race: A Study in Social Dynamics*. New York: Modern Reader Paperbacks, 1948.

Eisenkraft, Harriet. "Racism in the Academy." *UA/AU*, October 12, 2010. www.universityaffairs.ca/features/feature-article/racism-in-the-academy/.

Hamad, Ruby. *White Tears/Brown Scars: How White Feminism Betrays Women of Color*. New York: Catapult Press, 2020.

Jones-Rogers, Stephanie E. *They Were Her Property: White Women as Slave Owners in the American South*. New Haven, CT: Yale University Press, 2019.

Lee, Butch. *Jailbreak Out of History: The Re-Biography of Harriet Tubman and the Evil of Female Loaferism*. Montreal: Kersplebedeb, 2015.

Rajack-Talley, Theresa. "We Do Not Have to Be White or Men to Lead: Redefining and Assessing Black Women's Leadership." *Palimpsest: A Journal on Women, Gender, and the Black International* 10, no. 2 (2021): 205–14.

Smith, Daryl G. *Diversity's Promise for Higher Education: Making It Work*. Baltimore, MD: Johns Hopkins University Press, 2015.

Talley, Clarence. "The 'Race' Concept and Racial Structures." In *Living Racism: Through the Barrel of the Book*, edited by Theresa Rajack-Talley and Derrick Brooms, 11–28. Lanham, MD: Lexington Press, 2018.

Talley, Clarence, and Theresa Rajack-Talley. "Racial Etiquette and Racial Stereotypes." In *Living Racism: Through the Barrel of the Book*, edited by Theresa Rajack-Talley and Derrick Brooms, 51–76. Lanham, MD: Lexington Press, 2018.

Washington, Nuh. *All Power to the People*. Montreal: Arm the Spirit/Solidarity, 2002.

9

Hear My Prayer

*Embrace the Possibilities of
Leadership with Humility*

Colette M. Taylor

Special Assistant to the Provost for Strategic
Directions, Seattle University

I have embraced the idea instilled by my parents throughout my life and career that one can "learn from every experience." My parents and grandfather showed, told, and role-modeled that success was never a question of my ability but the application of everyday life lessons. As someone who found herself stepping into a department chair role at a modern, progressive, and global Jesuit Catholic university, despite promising myself never to return to an administrative position in higher education, I find it vital to pass on my story and what I learned from this experience. It is an important story filled with the highs and lows, the mistakes, and the lessons learned that you, the next generation of department chairs, might use as a catalyst to begin reimagining the possibilities of leadership roles for Black women in the academy.

Thus, I offer a part of St. Theresa's Prayer: "May you not forget the infinite possibilities that are born of faith in yourself and others. May you use the gifts that you have received and pass on the love that has been given to you."

My Story: *May You Not Forget the Infinite Possibilities That Are Born of Faith in Yourself*

At age fifty-two, I am a professor of educational and organizational learning and leadership and a Special Assistant to the Provost. Before taking on this new role, I spent two years as a department chair in the College of Education, undergoing tremendous change. After earning my doctorate in educational leadership, policy, and foundations from the University of Florida in 2003, I spent the first part of my career as a student affairs administrator, serving in a variety of administrative roles at Wake Forest University, Nova Southeastern University, University of Florida, and Middle Tennessee State University, respectively.

In 2008, I become an Assistant Professor of Higher Education at Texas Tech University. When I transitioned from student affairs administration to being a full-time faculty member, I envisioned a life focused on research, teaching, and writing, never wanting to return to a life of supervision and leadership. However, the promised lifestyle of the scholar never materialized. Despite my hopes of leaving administration behind, I was "voluntold" the opportunity to restructure the master's program in higher education and serve as Program Coordinator of the Graduate Certificate and Master's Program in Higher Education, due to my administrative skill set. I did this successfully and happily earned a promotion to Associate Professor with tenure in early 2014.

In 2015, I transitioned to Seattle University, where I once again hoped to focus solely on research, teaching, and writing. However, due to the departure of three senior faculty members, I was again thrust into a leadership role, where I had the opportunity to restructure the doctoral program and serve as the Program Director of Doctor of Education in Educational and Organizational Learning and Leadership. If you think you see a pattern, you are not wrong. I can never say no to a challenge.

With the upcoming organizational changes resulting from the selection of a new university president and College of Education dean, we needed a department chair with administrative experience who understood the realities and complexities of the higher education landscape. My previous experiences as a faculty member and administrator gave me insight into the ways in which the next department chair needed to be adaptable while working through situations related to our college's demanding, mission-critical nature. I finally decided to step into the role of Department Chair in the College of Education after being repeatedly asked to fill the chair position, which had been vacant for a year.

May You Use the Gifts That You Have Received: Reflections on My Experience

As I look back at this experience, there are several things I wish I had known that would have better prepared me to lead as an African American female department chair. Few individuals come into their roles as department chairs with the knowledge of what the job entails, such as managing departmental budgets, scheduling courses and meetings, and the mounds of forms and paperwork involved (Evans 2021). As chair, I had to be a strong advocate; a consensus builder; a budget wizard; and an extraordinary manager of people, tasks, and emotions in order to implement university policies and directives.

As a department chair, I often experienced stress as I walked a tightrope between serving the department and faculty and students and representing the central administration. I wish I had known about several important issues before I started the job. I hope my experiences can help new and future department chairs anticipate difficulties and better set themselves up for success in one of the most challenging roles on campus. Upon this reflection, here are my recommendations about leadership and management for success.

Remember Your Previous Life Lessons about Self-Care

At the institutions of higher learning that I've worked at, I have made valuable contributions both to the institutions and the students I served. I raced around working hard to establish my credibility as a leader, often to the detriment of my own well-being. In other words, I tried to be Black Superwoman. Superwoman is the savior needed to help the African American family and community survive, as described by the Strong Black Woman schema. "The SBW helps a Black woman to remain tenacious against dual oppressions of racism and sexism. It keeps her from falling victim to her own despair, but it also masks her vulnerabilities. As much as it may give her the illusion of control, it keeps her from identifying what she needs and reaching out for help" (Abrams, Hill, and Maxwell 2019, 517).

I needed to remember that trying to be Black Superwoman is not healthy. Like many women of color, I placed this job above my health. Many, many mentors have reminded me to "feed yourself before you feed others." I learned this the hard way. After being in the chair role for only four months, it took a serious health scare to remind me that self-care, whether physical or mental, is the most important. I counsel doctoral students and junior faculty not to let their careers be the only thing that defines them, but at the time, I exercised little, ate like a teenager, and obsessively checked email as if there were bonus points for how fast I could reply. I internalized each problem that arose as proof of my failure as chair. My health deteriorated as my blood pressure skyrocketed, and I had to make drastic lifestyle changes. This was a lesson I should have remembered from earlier in my career. Ironically, I'd published an article titled "Superwoman Lives (At Least in My Head): Reflections of a Mid-Level Professional in Student Affairs" (Taylor 2005), in which I write, "It occurred to me that I was so busy trying to prove myself to other people that I had forgotten one of the most valuable lessons my parents had taught me. This lesson was a challenge to create space for my life and build my priorities around my life, rather than trying to build my life around my priorities" (203). I had to practice what I taught! As a leadership educator, I train individuals to develop a personal leadership philosophy to get super clear on their values and commit to those values through personal goals and habits. The philosophy should guide your life whenever you have decisions to make in any area—whether career, relationships, or lifestyle. Revisiting my personal leadership plan reminded me of my priorities and helped me reset my direction and resist external pressure when others tried to redefine my priorities for me.

Do Not Accept Being Erased

While I anticipated a shift in my daily routine due to my new chair responsibilities, I was not always prepared for the shift in how faculty colleagues treated me as the only tenured African American faculty member in a department of sixteen full-time faculty. The department chair's work was extremely gratifying. Simultaneously, the work was thankless and exhausting, and it was easy to lose focus on my identity while addressing others' needs among the political and social pressures. Many faculty of color working in predominantly white spaces can, at times, face a chilling and hostile work environment. I readily identify as a heterosexual female who embraces my African American heritage. My social identity intersects with my research, teaching, and service endeavors. As an African American woman, I have struggled to name myself as both at the same time in my leadership roles. Despite earning tenure, being a stellar teacher, prolific researcher, and engaged community member, I consistently face microaggressions, racism, and sexism in my role as chair.

More often than not, colleagues have attempted to erase me from conversations where my perspectives made them either uncomfortable or accountable. If they did not like my requests for action, or my descriptions of expectations, or if I denied their requests for additional financial support, some department faculty members tried to go straight to the dean and erase me from the conversation. Sometimes in department or college-wide meetings, certain individuals, particularly white male colleagues, attempted to ignore anything I mentioned in discussions.

Crenshaw (1989) theorizes that Black women are rendered invisible within US institutions due to their multiple social identities, framed as either/or and not both. As an African American female chair, I have often faced this dilemma, am often forced to choose one or the other when advocating for racial and gender injustice. I have experienced bias and discrimination from individuals who should have known better. I have been "doubly marginalized," as Bell (1990) describes, in naming Black women's experiences with racism and sexism. When these identities are framed as isolated and mutually exclusive, it results in a theoretical erasure of Black women who hold multiple minoritized identities (Harris and Patton 2019, 347).

During this time of increased awareness of social injustice, our institutions have increased efforts to engage in conversations about honoring and respecting individuals from marginalized populations. At the same time, as I have been targeted at the intersection of being Black and being a woman, I still am expected to take care of everyone else by virtue of my identity and position. I cannot recall a week in the chair position where I did not experience double marginalization. As an African American woman, I am often expected to show deference to white women and/or men.

Now to be sure, I am not the only faculty member who has felt erased during these conversations, but in my role as chair, it was imperative to attempt to address these experiences. I discussed establishing ground rules so everyone knew how to engage and hold everyone to the same established standards. I required respectful language and attitudes from all participants. I tried very hard not to let anyone start laying blame—wanting to avoid "us vs. them" type of language, especially for hot-button issues like politics or racial dynamics. While I did not publicly call anyone out by name, I let it be known that misbehaviors would not be tolerated. Most importantly, I had a critical conversation with the dean at the time about the consequences of enabling this behavior, which created a toxic culture and could have easily led to legal liabilities. We reaffirmed good behaviors and developed strategies to hold individuals accountable for their harmful actions.

Understand the Power of Ho'oponopono

During a difficult time, I recognized that the department had been experiencing organizational harm, damage, trauma, and injustice during the last few years. As chair, it was up to me to help the department heal, replenish, restore efficacy and positive energy, and enhance resiliency. Fostering forgiveness is one effective mechanism for achieving those outcomes.

When we were exploring how to accomplish this difficult task, a beloved colleague reminded me of the Hawaiian approach to reparation, forgiveness, gratitude, and love. Simply translated, Ho'oponopono (Patten 1994) means "to make things rightly right," with ho'o meaning "to make" and pono meaning "right."

The practice involves openly expressing feelings, holding space for each other, exchanging particular words, and cleansing your consciousness. If your mind can have problematic thoughts, it can also solve them. Ho'oponopono is a Hawaiian technique of repeating four sentiments that can give you complete control over your life. When stressed, upset, and needing tools to recenter myself, I have found remembering the following four affirmations helpful: I am sorry, Forgive me, Thank you, and I love you.

Ho'oponopono teaches that negative feelings in the work environment are related to trauma from past experience connected to professional performance. I may have felt a colleague was not easy to work with or had harmed me somehow. Maybe I became embroiled in a blame game. Whatever the cause, holding grudges can cause exhaustion, isolation, and distraction from my actual goals. Ho'oponopono itself will not add happiness to my life, but it helps me let go of negative feelings. It brings me peace of mind.

Moreover, pass on the love that has been given to you.

Learn and Practice Leadership Humility

Most institutions appoint qualified people to terribly important positions but offer them little training and assistance. As Gmelch and Buller (2015) point out, "To put it bluntly, academic leadership is one of the few professions one can enter today with absolutely no training in, credentials for, or knowledge about the central duties of the position" (2). For me, having served as a higher education administrator for fifteen years before being a faculty member, I had the skills and experience to be a chair. At least, I thought I did. Having been an organizational leader before does not always translate to being an effective leader once appointed to a particular position.

Gist (2020) says of leaders in higher education, "They earned that recognition (and later promotion) by being expert at what they did—and carry into their new leadership role the desire to hold and display dominant expertise. This leads to being overwhelmed because the new leader's responsibilities have grown, and the desire to remain the expert interferes with delegation and developing others" (92). While I study and teach leadership theory and organizational change, I have had to remind myself to apply the theories to my daily practice once I accepted the chair appointment.

I was not prepared for faculty being less inclined to perceive the chair's role as one that represents central administration. Some of the faculty became outraged when I discussed departmental expectations and changes in the face of an institutional crisis, accusing me of "being an agent of the administration." Like many higher education institutions, my institution faced financial challenges, causing the Board of Trustees to charge a workgroup of faculty and staff to conduct an Academic Program Portfolio Review (APPR). This review would provide recommendations for the academic program offerings, enabling a transition to a portfolio that ensured mission fulfillment and financial sustainability. This meant working with each academic program to develop a proposal in response to new financial realities, which may have meant the closure of certain academic programs.

Almost immediately, I discovered that long-time faculty colleagues no longer believed that I was one of them. I became the "leadership," a euphemism for "I do not trust you, and you are THE MAN." I was challenged directly to find a way to engage the faculty in the process.

The Extraordinary Power of Leader Humility: Thriving Organizations—Great Results (Gist 2020) reframes the traditional domains of leadership and power often perceived through the filters of maleness and strength, by using dignity as an empowering translation for leadership. Leader humility is defined as "a tendency to feel and display a deep regard for others." As Gist reminds us, leaders with humility are aware of their strengths and accomplishments, but they focus more on the team's goals and others' contributions. By operating from this balance point, I managed my own ego rather than having my ego managed by my faculty. This was critically important for pulling "the team" together.

The faculty were experiencing significant stress and working in an exceptionally challenging environment. I sought to develop strong chair-faculty relationships to ease some of the pressure. Gist describes the development of these relationships as "a dance between my humility and your dignity. If I display regard for your dignity, then we're going to get along well, and you're going to feel comfortable. . . . [but] if I'm not sensitive to the fact that there's someone else I'm dancing with, then I might be stepping all over them" (quoted in Kislik 2020).

Respecting the dignity of others and acting from humility does not undermine leader effectiveness; it enhances it. Utilizing such skills is incredibly powerful because they help people feel seen. Moreover, when people feel seen and respected, they are much more likely to go the distance for you. Because of the pandemic, working from home, and the possibility of a significant change to the program, we were all feeling the strain. I began embracing humility to reshape my leadership and management practices. Leadership is about your ability to influence relationships, and humility is the foundation for all healthy relationships. Leader humility can increase engagement and retention by inspiring and motivating individuals to engage in the process.

Do Not Compromise Yourself

As leaders, department chairs face an incredible amount of pressure. Every day, we are asked to make decisions that may not have a clear right or wrong answer. Even our "best" solutions can come from a shortsighted place, reaping uncalculated consequences. As a chair, I know that my positive, team-centered attitude and constant drive to produce solid results provided a constructive advantage when I stepped into this role. But as a leader, I compromise. Compromise is particularly necessary at times of high tension. I sometimes compromise when negotiating a teaching assignment, working with colleagues on curriculum revisions, or resolving conflicts between students, faculty, or staff. All relationships, whether personal or professional, require compromise.

In leadership positions, compromise can carry a negative connotation tied to weakness and a sense of loss. Certain compromises happen at the core of who we are; they break down *self*, devaluing our sense of worth and piercing our confidence. Compromise of *self* looks like making decisions that defy one's value system, honor, or dignity. Whether it is meant to or not, compromising yourself depreciates your principles and discounts your moral standing. This type of compromise leads to cognitive dissonance, anxiety, and risk.

Each of us is uniquely valuable in our own right. By first understanding our self-worth, we can begin to operate in a state of mind rooted in personal values and not the leadership role. Leadership starts from within. Living a life without compromise of self leads to confidence, high self-esteem, and honor. However, not compromising yourself does not exempt you from practicing leadership humility. Reimagine your leadership style as a department chair by practicing leadership through situational awareness and empathy. Be confident enough to have interpersonal humility. Strong leaders know they do not have all the answers and genuinely value others. Strong leaders respect the dignity of everyone around them—no matter the individual's status—inviting ideas, truth-telling, and collaboration. Humility in leadership is powerful: take the time to understand others, their needs, and what you can do to help them.

One Final Thought

There is a balance to leadership when we dismiss our self-importance and see ourselves as no better or more important than the faculty members we lead. When I eventually leave this office for what I hope will be a higher-level administrative opportunity, I want my legacy to be that I fostered a positive, inviting, respectful, and inclusive work environment that allowed my faculty, students, and staff to succeed in all their endeavors.

As a reader and scholar, you have the right to dismiss all that I have told you to this point; but I implore you to hear my modification of St. Theresa's prayer:

> May you embrace the infinite possibilities that are born of faith in yourself and others.
> May you re-examine past experiences for new lessons to guide your present.
> May you not allow yourself to be erased while helping others respectively embrace your presence.

May you practice Ho'oponopono to apologize, forgive, thank, and love.

May you lead with humility and be empathic, compassionate, supportive, and engaging.

May you use this wisdom to strengthen yourself for the leadership ahead and pass on the love that has been given to you.

References

Abrams, Jasmine A., Ashley Hill, and Morgan Maxwell. "Underneath the Mask of the Strong Black Woman Schema: Disentangling Influences of Strength and Self-Silencing on Depressive Symptoms among U.S. Black Women." *Sex Roles* 80 (2019): 517–26.

Bell, Ella L. "The Bicultural Life Experience of Career-Oriented Black Women." *Journal of Organizational Behavior* 11, no. 6 (1990): 459–77.

Crenshaw, Kimberlé. "Demarginalizing the Intersection of Race and Sex: A Black Feminist Critique of Antidiscrimination Doctrine, Feminist Theory and Antiracist Politics." *University of Chicago Legal Forum* 1989, no. 1 (1989): 139–67.

Dillon, Maureen. "14 of the Most Powerful Peace Quotes from St Teresa of Avila." *Cora Evans Blog*. n.d. www.coraevans.com/blog/article/14-Of-The -Most-Powerful-Peace-Quotes-From-St-Teresa-Of-Avila.

Domingue, Andrea D. "'Our Leaders Are Just We Ourself': Black Women College Student Leaders' Experiences with Oppression and Sources of Nourishment on a Predominantly White College Campus." *Equity & Excellence in Education* 48, no. 3 (2015): 454–72.

Evans, Stephanie Y. "Meditations from a Black Woman Chair: Social Justice Values and a New Normal in Academic Administration." *The Department Chair* 32, no. 1 (Summer 2021): 12–15. https://doi.org/10.1002/dch.30395.

Gist, Marilyn. *The Extraordinary Power of Leader Humility: Thriving Organizations—Great Results*. Oakland, CA: Berrett-Koehler Publishers, Inc., 2020.

Gmelch, Walter H., and Jeffrey L. Buller. *Building Academic Leadership Capacity: A Guide to Best Practices*. San Francisco: Jossey-Bass, 2015.

Harris, Jessica C., and Lori D. Patton. "Un/Doing Intersectionality Through Higher Education Research." *Journal of Higher Education* 90, no. 3 (2019): 347–72.

Kislik, Liz. "How to Build Humility, the Magic Ingredient in Leaders' Success." *Forbes*, November 5, 2020. www.forbes.com/sites/lizkislik/2020/11/05/how-to-build-humility-the-magic-ingredient-in-leaders-success/?sh=6f5b9ab34479.

Patten, Thomas H. "Ho'oponopono: A Cross-Cultural Model for Organizational Development and Change." *International Journal of Organizational Analysis* 2, no. 3 (1994): 252–63.

Taylor, Colette M. "And the Tree Is Not Always Happy!: A Black Woman Authentically Leading and Teaching Social Justice in Higher Education." In *Black Women and Social Justice Education: Legacies and Lessons*, edited by Stephanie Y. Evans, Andrea D. Domingue, and Tania D. Mitchell, 219–29. Albany, NY: SUNY Press, 2019.

———. "Superwoman Lives (at Least in My Head): Reflections of a Mid-Level Professional in Student Affairs." *College Student Affairs Journal* 24, no. 2 (Spring 2005): 201–3.

10

Pulling the Table to My Chair at EMU

Eunice Myles Jeffries

Board Chair, Eastern Michigan University

This commentary is dedicated to Dr. Chiara Hensley, who no doubt would have been the very first person that I would have consulted when I received this invitation. I recognized her passion and impact in higher education and at Eastern Michigan University in the very early days of my term as regent. She would attend the Educational Policy committee meetings, always sitting to my right. The way she would lean in and engage always captured my attention, even in my periphery. Whenever I looked toward her, her encouraging smile and nod of approval were assuring and comforting to me. Dr. Hensley left on a medical leave that proved quite serious, with a grim prognosis. I could not wait for her return to work, as I had so much to discuss with her. I wanted and needed to pick her brain, to glean insight from her and plan with her about the greatness we could achieve together on the strength of student empowerment. Dr. Hensley was our Assistant Vice President of Academic and Student Affairs in title. In action, she was a constant leader, helping students find their way, with a passion for issues of race and gender equity and inclusion and universal education. When I became Board Chair, I knew that no one would have been more excited than Dr. Chiara Hensley. This is for you, gone but never forgotten. I miss you.

Dear Board Chair:

Congratulations to you! It has already been a multiyear journey for you to even get to this point, but get ready because the rocket ship ride has just begun, believe it or not. You have either run for elective office or have been appointed by the governor. You've served as a board member or committee chair, endured many meetings, met so many people, led a major fundraising effort, survived an unfavorable news story about the institution that felt like it would never go away, welcomed new students to campus at move-in, celebrated with families at every commencement, and were elected by your colleagues on the board to lead the next phase of this voluntary journey. Now, here you are, gavel in hand and all eyes on you! Just like your journey to becoming the chair of the board, there is no set path or instruction manual that encompasses your role in this leadership post. The Association of Governing Boards (AGB) is a great resource of articles, publications, and conferences for all board members. *The Principles of Trusteeship*, published by AGB, is a must-read for every board member and a must-re-read and frequent reference for the board chair. The range and scope of the actual duties of board chair can only be discovered on the job, and they are humbling, empowering, frustrating, challenging, enlightening, encouraging, discouraging, tiring, and exuberating all at the same time, and board chair happens to earn double the pay of board member (wink). I assure you that your institution needs you and needs what you uniquely have to offer in this role. It is your time to serve.

Board Chair? Really? But How?

My journey to becoming the first African American woman to lead the Board of Regents at Eastern Michigan University consisted of (and still necessitates) celebration, preparedness, collaboration, damn good mentoring, and timing, to be honest. I wish I could say that I wrote my goals down, made a plan, and worked the plan. That would be misleading in a big way. I have always been concerned with having a good reputation, making sure my word is bond and being someone that people can trust. My background is in government and community relations; I've worked for four statewide-elected officials. My value is in my reputation and my rolodex, or as they say in 2021, my contacts. I didn't know it then but I was creating my "personal brand." Jeff Bezos came up with the term first, I'm told, but I first heard it from Carla Harris, Vice Chairman, Managing Director, and Senior Client Advisor at Morgan Stanley, via a TED Talk.

What Harris says about your personal brand is this: "it is what people are saying about you when you are not in the room." I truly believe this is what happened sometime back in 2016, as appointments to the Eastern Michigan University Board of Regents came up on the agenda in the governor's office. Things were said about me in that room that made me a good fit at the time for the university board, and none of us saw it coming, including folks at EMU. My eight-year appointment became effective January 1, 2017, and will end December 30, 2024. Being a regent or university board member is an incredible honor and it never gets old. I found it intimidating and an honor all at once. I already felt intimidated, and then there were those around me who underestimated me and I knew it. Most university board appointments can be tied to some obvious connection, alumni, financer, or high-profile individual. The reasoning behind appointing me just wasn't that obvious to many.

Board members usually serve as Chair of the Board in years seven and eight, just as they complete the term. I happen to be serving in years five and six of my term, with two years to go after my chairmanship. The timing of board terms and dynamics surrounding other board members created a unique and timely opportunity to run for chair, so I ran! Succession planning is incredibly important in order to make sure that the chair is prepared to lead on day one of the chairmanship. At Eastern Michigan University, the chair is prepared in three ways: by shadowing the Board Chair in key meetings and on communications, by serving as Chair of the Finance Committee working closely with the Chief Financial Officer, and by serving as Vice Chair of the Board. The purpose is to provide stability in leadership and exposure to what the role entails. There was one small unexpected set of circumstances on the horizon of my impending rise to become chair . . . a global pandemic. No playbook, no end in sight, and endless questions greeted the start of my term as chair in 2020, in addition to the other pressures that come with the position.

Reporting for Duty!

Other institutions of higher education established by law having authority to grant baccalaureate degrees shall each be governed by a board of control which shall be a body corporate. The board shall have general supervision of the institution and the control and direction of all expenditures from the institution's funds. It shall, as often as necessary, elect a president of the institution under its supervision. He shall be the principal executive officer of the institution and be ex-officio a member of the board without the right to vote. The board may elect one of its members or may designate the president to preside at board meetings. Each board of control shall consist of eight members who shall hold office for terms of eight years, not more than two of which shall expire in the same year, and who shall be appointed by the governor by and with the advice and consent of the Senate. Vacancies shall be filled in like manner.

—Michigan Constitution of 1963 (ratified 1964), Article 8.

This is fancy talk to say that the board of regents has a responsibility to be stewards of the finances of the university and to hire and fire the president. Each institution organizes differently but the roles come with the same challenges regardless, due to the nature of higher education and how it is funded here in Michigan. Public universities depend heavily on state government for funding, and unfortunately, higher education has not felt like it is a priority here in Michigan. Notice how the statute itself refers to the president of the institution as *he*? Very telling about institutions and their leadership back in 1963. Colleges and universities have a ways to go in supporting women in leadership roles, and even further to go in relation to Black women in leadership—the very premise for this book! There have been times in my role as chair that I have been unable to identify exactly which *"ism"* I am facing. Is it racism, sexism, or ageism? (I happen to be fairly young to be board chair in comparison to my predecessors, and in comparison to the current president, who is about fifteen years my senior.) I don't think I will ever get the answer to that question, but the biases went beyond implicit bias, if you ask me—at times, it has been quite obvious.

Major Challenges

I have found that the major challenges concern funding, campus safety surrounding Title IX and rising incidents of gun violence in public spaces, labor contracts, and enrollment. Of course there are others, but for the role of the board, these areas are the most sobering after all the fanfare of becoming a board member and ultimately becoming chair. Finances and funding have always been a concern to me, not only on behalf of Eastern Michigan University but also on behalf of our students and their families in terms of the costs they are expected to cover themselves. I find that the "EFC" (estimated family contribution) on a student's FAFSA is not reflective of reality for the student or the family (maybe I'm wrong here but I don't think so). It is a challenge to achieve the right tuition price point that is reflective of the educational experience and is affordable. Regardless of how the board is organized (through a committee system or otherwise), it's essential to understand the finances of the institution, the size of the endowment, the financial aid budget, and how they intersect.

Another challenge that you have already come to know, especially if you've been elected chair of the board, involves some personality management of your colleagues. Oftentimes, this is a delicate balance. We all serve on the board for different reasons and have different interests and priorities. I respect all of my colleagues and appreciate their expertise and insight on various matters, but our students' best interests must always come first. As chair, you will sometimes find yourself in the middle of conflicting opinions and priorities among your colleagues after hearing or reading the very same data. I have found it best to keep the best interests of the students and campus community as my north star. Personality management can become dicey at times if you let it, so don't let it. As a Black woman, I am all too familiar with feeling not heard, not taken seriously, or not represented at times in professional settings, which causes me to lead from a position of inclusion and respect for all of my colleagues, and to attempt to exercise great patience. Remember that board members are appointed by the governor and confirmed by the state senate. Regents come to the board with impressive credentials, notable accomplishments, and a built-in inclination to lead, and there will be personality clashes! As chair, it's important to stay above the fray and focus on leading and supporting the president and his/her administration on behalf of the students.

Lessons Learned

Lesson #1: **Step up and step out on faith: Learn the craft.** When asked a question, answer it truthfully. The question was asked among my colleagues who had plans for pursuing a greater role on the board and exactly what was the greater role being pursued? In other words, someone interested in running for board chair wanted to know who else was interested in running. The question was meant to smoke out the competition for the position. At that point I had no plans to run for chair in the next two years, but when I heard the way the question was posed, and knowing that there were some who didn't believe I had enough experience to lead the board, my spirit spoke for me. I said something like, "I absolutely have interest in leading this board someday." That simple reply determined my trajectory. I became Chair of the Finance Committee, which at EMU is the traditional path for board members to become board chair.

Lesson #2: **Take the bitter with the sweet.** Don't take anything personally. Higher education itself can be political, and the higher up within the organization, the more political things can become. Everyone has an agenda and will view you as an ally or as an obstacle. It's never personal. It is about the agenda of the other party. Taking things personally will cause you to appear weak and will distract you from being an effective leader. I learned this lesson the hard way. I thought people were hot, then cold, with me because of their expectations of me as a regent. In reality, people play "the game" with regents based on the position, not the person holding the title. If you're new to the role, this may not be obvious up front. It is a learned understanding. Some will love you because you are a regent and some won't for the very same reason. It is not personal.

Lesson #3: **Own your right to be at the table and move beyond self-defeating attitudes.** It took me about a year to realize that my voice was just as important as the other seven regents around the table. When I was appointed to the board, I felt disadvantaged in relation to my colleagues. I am not an alumna. I had no professional higher education experience and I certainly was not a major donor. I was also at a much different station in life than the others on the board. I was not an executive or a business owner and was in middle management of a very large organization. In essence, I was a small fish in a big pond, but was a very big fish in a small pond off-hours as a regent. I had to work hard to get past that self-defeating thinking (stinking thinking). I often reflect back to a meeting with the governor. His speech on inspiring college and university board members to lead and do it boldly ended up really inspiring me. He said, "I know you can do it because I appointed you and I did it because I knew you were right for the job." Those words did something to me. I had to fight tears while sitting in that room with all these leaders in education. It was at that moment that I finally owned and embraced the fact that indeed I was one of them. Lesson learned—I belong here!

Lesson #4: **Start at ground zero.** I also had to learn how to ask the right questions. University officials, administrators, directors, the executive council, deans, and fundraisers across the entire institution have the clear advantage of knowing the inner workings of higher education and the institution far better than the board. They are in it day to day—they see it, feel it, manage it. Oftentimes, information is presented in such a way to try and set the agenda and priorities for the board; it's called managing up and we all do it. Well, I learned that we must ask very intentional and direct questions with our own lens, which may be a lens of diversity, or of industry, within a particular workforce, or station in life, or worldview. Know what questions to ask that will render the feedback you are searching for. It's healthy for the administration to have a multidimensional perspective, and it is your duty to bring your perspective to the board.

Lesson #5: **Live in the work: Public and private.** As regent and as board chair, I have learned that the job is round the clock and people who know you are a university leader will always see you as such. I remember driving on a Saturday morning and becoming frustrated with another motorist. I wasn't kind in what I had to say, and one of my children said, "Ok, Regent Jeffries." I learned in that moment that even though people act like they aren't paying attention, guess what? They not only are paying attention but see you in your role even when you are not officially serving in that role. You represent the institution and must always represent it well. Remember, this is about your personal branding as well, not just the brand of the institution (though that's very important).

Lesson #6: **You don't have to do this job, you get to do this job.** I have learned that regardless of the size of the institution, makeup of the student body, size of the endowment, whether the board is elected or appointed, or what athletic conference you are in (Eastern Michigan University is in the MAC—Mid-American Conference), we all face the same sort of challenges as leaders. Some may have more resources to deal with them, but across all boards, we share the same concerns. Publications like *Trusteeship Magazine*, published by the Association of Governing Boards, give evidence of this, and I've seen it when I spend time with other college and university leaders. Realizing this important lesson will help you lead your institution with the pride that it deserves, regardless of the other institutions in the area. You share the same struggles but on different scales of economy.

Recommendations for Leadership and Efficacy

As a board chair, I would recommend you lead the board first and the university second. It is important that the board has one voice and it is a collective one. The old saying "we can all sing together but we can't all talk together" is applicable when leading a governing body. Before scheduling that one-on-one with the president and setting your agenda, take the time to do that with your colleagues on the board. They have demonstrated their trust in you to be their voice and to represent them—honor the trust by investing the time early on. A board can support you or it can turn on you rather quickly. I have seen it happen at other institutions.

All members of the board should come to meetings prepared. Read the materials beforehand and be ready to discuss them at the meetings. I know this can be difficult because there is so much information to process that weighs heavily on the quality of discussions and decisions that will be made. Thoroughly reading the material shows respect to the college or university employees that took the time to prepare the information and assemble it for you. This is an opportunity to showcase the work product coming from your areas, to celebrate accomplishments, and to show respect to other board members, as well as to make sure you are informed about what's going on at the department and college level. It is apparent if you haven't read the materials and you end up losing credibility when you are not prepared. It's even worse when you are not prepared but try to come across like you are. Academicians can spot the bull a mile away.

Be transparent with your colleagues on the board and be someone they can trust. It is a high honor to serve as a college or university board member and the best way to maintain the honor is to be honorable among your own colleagues. You don't have to always agree, and if you do, that's a bit of a red flag—no one agrees on everything. You should always, however, be able to trust one another and speak with one another, or at the bare minimum with your board chair, before speaking with the administration. The employees will respect you and your colleagues will too. As board chair, you will hear about the side conversations anyway. It always gets back. Do yourself a favor and respect the protocol and your colleagues on the board.

Know the difference between leading and managing and when to "move." As a board member, you are charged with empowering, delegating, being a resource, and leading. Managing tasks, no matter how good you are at it, is not the place for any member of the board. Sometimes it is hard to resist, but remember, just as in your career and in your personal life, failures and misfires helped shape you into the leader you are today. Plus, remember how you were bothered when your boss or that one co-worker didn't stay in their lane and tried to manage what you were doing? Don't be that board member. Allow the president and the president's cabinet to manage the process; playing a leading and supporting role is enough.

Serving on the board of a university, you can get caught up in enrollment numbers, the budget, housing costs, audits, sports scheduling, headlines, presidential searches, diversity numbers—the list goes on and on if you allow it. Appreciate the human capital of it all and get to know the students: all the students, not just the ones on the dean's list. I advise getting to know the ones on and off academic probation, the ones that took a gap year or are taking six years to complete their degree, and the students that are just getting by. Listen to their stories and you will be inspired. We work for them. Commencement is met with great fanfare, but we work for the ones barely holding on too. As leaders in our respective fields, we know best that grades are not always a predictor of success. My transcripts are an example of this. Students, faculty, and staff keep me going. I enjoy learning their stories, where they are from, what their major is, and why they selected Eastern Michigan University. Take the time to take it all in. Our college campuses are beautiful on the outside and inside. Well-manicured buildings donning the school colors reflect the spirit of the place, but the inside is a mosaic of the very fiber of humanity and we get to access and enjoy it.

My last recommendation would be that when your time has ended as board member and/or board chair, please allow the next leaders to do their jobs and lead. As a former board member, your job is to mentor, be an ambassador, be a donor (if you're able), and show immense pride and support for the institution and the leaders. Continuing to interact with the administration after your term puts the university employees in potentially awkward positions that test their loyalty, which should be with the current board members. Always remember to praise in public and correct in private! I'm sure you have experienced those with emeritus status that still call up the president, the chief financial officer, the provost, the athletic director, or their favorite peer that is still on the board. This undermines your authority, so don't do it to your successors. There is a role for you, but it must be appropriate. Remember, you served your time and although you will become a former regent, that is still a small and very elite group!

Once again, congratulations to you, Madam or Mr. Chair: welcome to the club. Your leadership is needed right now, for whatever the university is facing. And thanks very much for your service. You will be great!

Afterword

*A Letter from Dr. Tracy Sharpley-Whiting,
Co-Chair of Chair at the Table Project,
Vice Provost for Arts and Libraries,
Vanderbilt University*

Dear Colleagues,

As I close out this volume, I want to commend the editors for this essential work that strategically frames the experiences of Black women leaders in the academy. The epistolary genre provides for a certain intimacy and connection. Used effectively, as it is here, it allows Black women to tell their leadership stories while simultaneously offering usable tools to readers as they contemplate their leadership pathways. Martin Luther King, Jr. uses the form to significant effect in "Letter from Birmingham Jail," as does James Baldwin with *The Fire Next Time*. And while Harriet Jacobs crafted her story of bondage and escape to freedom as a series of "incidents," she occasionally deploys the supplicant "Dear Reader" to close the gap between her lived experiences and those of readers, to impart a sort of "quiet as it's kept" didacticism.

My path to leadership began first as a chair of French, followed by stints as director and chair of Black Studies. I was content to stay at this level of academic leadership, as it allowed me the freedom to continue a robust research program and, later, to be very present when my daughter was born in 2002. I had declined overtures from the previous administration about senior academic positions. Thus, I was slightly stunned when the Vice Provost of Faculty Affairs asked me to join her team as the Associate Vice Provost of Academic Advancement in October 2021. I requested a few days to think it over. In the past, whenever she asked me to serve on various committees, I always obliged. I thought her phone call would be another committee request. We arrived at Vanderbilt the same year and served on the university's Promotions, Tenure, and Review Committee (PTRC). We also shared the same first name (hers spelled Tracey with an "e"), the same place (Missouri), and year of birth. She was in the Law School, and I was in Arts and Science. The point here is that *relationships matter*. We had a history together that began through serendipitous service to the university. I trusted her, and she is, to this day, a *peer mentor*. Her timing was fortuitous, as it related to my openness to leadership change and my daughter had left for college. Vanderbilt hired a new chancellor in 2020, from the University of Chicago, and a provost in July 2021 from New York University. I learned subsequently that the provost had explicitly asked the Vice Provost of Faculty Affairs to identify someone firm yet diplomatic; someone who was well-respected among the faculty and had unimpeachable scholarly credentials, as this new role was primarily tied to external academic review and would require interfacing with deans and with prolific scholars from peer institutions who were also members of various national academies; someone who would get things done (a "doer," she said) and who, most importantly, was conversant across multiple disciplines.

Unlike chairs in the traditional disciplines, I cannot emphasize enough how those of us in Black Studies have had to be knowledgeable of other fields of study, a trademark of our interdisciplinarity. The chair of English does not need to understand the scholarly criteria of sociology; their direct exposure to that discipline might come through service on a school or university-level review and retention committee. But the chair or program director of Black Studies, who might also be an English professor, certainly needs to know about sociology because our unit hires come from multiple disciplines. From that vantage point, chairs and directors in Black Studies are particularly positioned for deanships and provost-level appointments, given their bird's-eye view of the academic ecosystem. Even if our faculty numbers are smaller, our knowledge base must be broad. And I want to say that if you are currently leading a Black Studies program or department and aspire to other administrative ranks at your institution or beyond, you need to begin in earnest making this unique skill set legible by *talking about it* to your dean as you map out pathways to senior leadership. It would help if you also considered lobbying for a seat on the school or university-level tenure and promotion committee or other high-level trans-disciplinary awards committees requiring peer letters to ensure that legibility further. Service on a board of scholarly associations, particularly elected positions, provides external leadership skills and enlarges your footprint and profile. These association positions represent an external imprimatur. I served as president of the Association of Departments of Foreign Languages and Literatures and on the Executive Council of the Modern Language Association.

After I'd served nine months as associate provost, the provost decided that as an institution in a city known for its creative industries and referred to as Music City, the university needed to signal its commitment to the creative economy more explicitly. She then promoted me to Vice Provost for Arts and Libraries in July 2022. With that promotion came a chief budget officer, dedicated support staff, multimillion-dollar budget responsibilities, and close to two hundred reporting personnel. Now I'd like to pivot and conclude with a story that encompasses the leadership strategies that have served me well. I hope they will, whether you are already a senior-level leader or an aspiring one, in some small way help you become the senior academic leader you aspire to be.

I live in the city of Nashville, in an urban, mixed-use neighborhood, where the main boulevard is lined with lush trees and large, older homes of varying distinct architectural styles: four squares, Queen Annes, bungalows, etc. While Vanderbilt University is within walking distance from my house, Belmont University dominates this part of the city. So do steep hills. At 6 a.m., at least three or four times a week, I like to tackle those hills as part of my exercise routine.

I selected a particularly steep hill near Belmont's Fisher Center for Performing Arts as my challenge. The goal: running up the hill to the top without becoming winded. Accustomed to using a resistance machine like the Bowflex, I decided to supplement my "Flo-Jo" routine with free weights. And then, I got a little overzealous and injured my lower back. Grounded and disappointed, I used the next few days of recovery to plot how to still conquer the hill. I knew I could not run the hill as before because I didn't want to aggravate the injury further. I turned to my partner, who suggested a way to modify my workout. So, I began to walk the hill on my toes. I felt a little like a preening peacock. And yet, I achieved similar cardiovascular intensity and anaerobic benefits to my calves, glutes, and hamstrings.

Final Leadership Takeaways

Willingness to shift focus: I had become so fixated on running the hill that I couldn't initially see another path to my goal. In rethinking my routine, I weighed the reinjury risks and, in the end, I took a calculated risk that paid off. I encourage you to think about those obstacles to your goals, to write them down, and to remap your course to best serve your leadership goals.

Activate people: I've exercised seriously for the better part of thirty-five years. Sometimes, we think we know all there is to know, particularly about our bodies, ourselves, and what works. But it was my partner, who continues to exercise like he is still an Olympic-qualifying athlete, who helped me think differently. As leaders, we must remember to activate those who have trod the road we're on with great success and not be afraid to look vulnerable by enlisting them in problem-solving.

Keep perspective about failures: When my first strategy failed, I tried another because I kept my perspective on the end goal—physical fitness. Resiliency is critical to effective leadership. Your response to failure shapes you as much as your successes. How you repurpose your failure—and we will all have them—is critical to your growth as a leader.

Amitiés,
T. Denean Sharpley-Whiting

Contributor Bios

STEPHANIE G. ADAMS, PHD, is the Erik Jonsson School of Engineering and Computer Science Dean and Lars Magnus Ericsson Chair in Electrical Engineering at the University of Texas at Dallas, and a past President of the American Society of Engineering Education. Previously Dr. Adams served as the Dean of the Frank Batten College of Engineering and Technology at Old Dominion University (2016–2019) and Department Head and Professor of Engineering Education at Virginia Tech (2011–2016). She also held faculty and administrative positions at Virginia Commonwealth University (2008–2011) and the University of Nebraska-Lincoln (1998–2008). Her research interests include broadening participation, faculty and graduate student development, international/global education, teamwork and team effectiveness, and quality control and management. In 2003, she received the CAREER award from the Engineering Education and Centers Division of the National Science Foundation. Dr. Adams is a leader in the advancement and inclusion of all in STEM education. She has worked with a number of colleges and universities, government agencies, and nonprofit organizations on topics related to graduate education, mentoring, faculty development, and diversifying STEM. Dr. Adams is an honor graduate of North Carolina A&T State University, where she earned her BS in mechanical engineering in 1988. In 1991, she was awarded the Master of Engineering degree in systems engineering from the University of Virginia. She received her PhD in interdisciplinary engineering from Texas A&M University in 1998, where she concentrated on industrial engineering and management.

JOHNNETTA BETSCH COLE, PHD, became Spelman College's seventh president in 1987, and the first Black woman to lead this college founded specifically for the education of women of African descent. Born in 1936 in Florida, Dr. Cole started her higher education at the age of fifteen, with early admission to Fisk University. She would later transfer to and graduate from Oberlin College in 1957. She earned her master's and doctorate degrees in anthropology from Northwestern University in 1959 and 1967. She held teaching positions at several schools including Washington State University, the University of Massachusetts Amherst, and Hunter College, where she was Professor of Anthropology and Director of the Latin American and Caribbean Studies Program until her departure in 1987, when she took the helm of Spelman College. After a decade of service to Spelman, Dr. Cole remained in Atlanta while returning to the classroom at Emory University as the Presidential Distinguished Professor of Anthropology, Women's Studies, and African-American Studies. In 2002, she became the president of Bennett College in North Carolina, the only other HBCU solely dedicated to educating Black women. She retired in 2007 and continued to serve as chair of the Johnnetta Betsch Cole Global Diversity and Inclusion Institute in Atlanta. In 2009, she was named director of the Smithsonian's National Museum of African Art, a position she currently holds.

STEPHANIE Y. EVANS, PHD, is Full Professor of Black Women's Studies at Georgia State University, appointed in Women's, Gender, and Sexuality Studies and as affiliate faculty in the Department of Africana Studies. She served as a department chair for twelve consecutive years at Georgia State University, Clark Atlanta University, and University of Florida. Her research interests are Black women's intellectual history, memoirs, and mental health. She is author of three books: *Black Women's Yoga History: Memoirs of Inner Peace* (SUNY Press, 2021); *Black Passports: Travel Memoirs as a Tool for Youth Empowerment* (SUNY Press, 2014); and *Black Women in the Ivory Tower, 1850–1954: An Intellectual History* (University Press of Florida, 2007), in addition to numerous journal articles. She is lead co-editor of four books: *Black Women and Public Health: Regenerative History, Practice, and Planning* (SUNY Press, 2022); *Black Women and Social Justice Education* (SUNY Press, 2019); *Black Women's Mental Health: Balancing Strength and Vulnerability* (SUNY Press, 2017); and *African Americans and Community Engagement in Higher Education* (SUNY Press, 2009). Dr. Evans is the curator of online resources including the Black Women's Studies Booklist, Africana Memoirs Database, Black Women's Music Database, Black Women's

Yoga History, and Africana Tea Network websites. She is editor of the *Black Women's Wellness* book series at SUNY Press. She is founder and co-chair of the Chair at the Table peer mentoring research collective.

TIFFANY GILBERT, PHD, is Chair and Associate Professor of the Department of English at the University of North Carolina Wilmington, where she teaches primarily in the areas of post-1945 American literature, film, and popular culture. She graduated with a BA in English from the College of William and Mary in 1993. In 1997, she earned a MA in English from Clemson University. She received her PhD in English from the University of Virginia in 2005. At UNCW, she co-directs the 1898 Legacies and Futures Research Collective, an initiative that nurtures the creation of constructive dialogue, innovative pedagogies, and new partnerships to advance ongoing remembrance and restoration efforts taking place throughout Wilmington and the Cape Fear region. She is currently co-editing a volume of essays, *The 1898 Wilmington Massacre: Critical Explorations on Insurrection, Black Resilience, and Black Futures*, contracted with Louisiana State University Press.

CAROL E. HENDERSON, PHD, is Vice Provost for Diversity and Inclusion, Chief Diversity Officer, and Advisor to the President at Emory University in Atlanta, Georgia. Henderson is responsible for leading the institution's DEI efforts. Prior to this appointment, she served as the inaugural Vice Provost for Diversity at the University of Delaware. During her tenure in that role, she led the university in a DEI strategic planning process, which garnered three institutional awards: a 2017 SHRM D & I Gold Award (co-winner), and two Insight into Diversity HEED Awards in 2017 and 2018. Before her appointment as Vice Provost for Diversity, Henderson also served as Associate Director/Director of Undergraduate Studies of then Black American Studies, and subsequently became the first chair of the department. Henderson has spent over twenty-five years in higher education. She is the recipient of several community, professional, and research awards; is the author or editor of five books and the special issue editor of four journals; and has published numerous essays in critical volumes and journals.

RÉGINE MICHELLE JEAN-CHARLES, PhD, is Dean's Professor of Culture and Social Justice; Director of Africana Studies; and Professor in the Department of Cultures, Societies, and Global Studies and the Women, Gender, and Sexuality Studies Program at Northeastern University. Dr. Jean-Charles is a Black feminist literary scholar and cultural critic who works at the intersection of race, gender, and justice. Her scholarship and teaching in Africana Studies include expertise on Black France, Sub-Saharan Africa, Caribbean literature, Black girlhood, Haiti, and the diaspora. She is the author of *Conflict Bodies: The Politics of Rape Representation in the Francophone Imaginary* (Ohio State University Press, 2014); *Martin Luther King and The Trumpet of Conscience Today* (Orbis Press, 2021); and *Looking for Other Worlds: Black Feminism and Haitian Fiction* (University of Virginia Press, 2022).

EUNICE MYLES JEFFRIES, MBA, is the first African American female Chair of the Board of Regents at Eastern Michigan University. Jeffries received her BS in accounting and business administration from Fisk University in Nashville, Tennessee, and received her MBA from Northwood University in Midland, Michigan. In addition, she is the Regent Representative on the EMU Foundation Board of Trustees and is a member of the Board of Regents Personnel and Compensation Committee. Her eight-year term appointment goes until December 2024. Jeffries is employed in higher education as well as Director of Government and Community Relations at Oakland Community College. In this role she leads the legislative and advocacy efforts of the college as well providing support to the community through sponsorships and engagement activities.

JULIA S. JORDAN-ZACHERY, PhD, is Chair and Professor of Women's, Gender, and Sexuality Studies at Wake Forest University. Jordan-Zachery is a leading voice on Black feminism and public policy, having published six books within the field including *Erotic Testimonies: Black Women Daring to Be Wild and Free* (SUNY Press, 2022) and *Shadow Bodies: Black Women, Ideology, Representation, and Politics* (Rutgers University Press, 2017). She co-edited *Black Girl Magic Beyond the Hashtag: Twenty-First-Century Acts of*

Self-Definition (University of Arizona Press, 2019) and *Black Political Women: Demanding Citizenship, Challenging Power, and Seeking Justice* (SUNY Press, 2018). Her first publication, *Black Women, Cultural Images, and Social Policy* (Routledge, 2010), won the W. E. B. Du Bois Best Book Award from the National Conference of Black Political Scientists and the Anna Julia Cooper Outstanding Book Publication Award by the Association for the Study of Black Women in Politics.

Sandra Jowers-Barber, PhD, is Division Director of Humanities and Criminology at the University of the District of Columbia Community College. Her research focuses on documenting the history of the deaf community. She looks at historical, social, and educational issues that have challenged and changed disability communities, with a focus on deafness. Her primary research project considers issues surrounding how "voice and empowerment" are given to this marginalized group. Her work includes exploring oral and public history, coordinating and facilitating community and family oral history projects, creating history curriculum, and writing and researching Black deaf history.

April Langley, PhD, is Chair and Associate Professor of African American Studies and Associate Professor of English at the University of South Carolina. She is also Associate Professor Emerita at the University of Missouri-Columbia, where she was Chair of the Department of Black Studies and Associate Professor of English and Black Studies. Langley specializes in eighteenth- and nineteenth-century African American and American literature and theory. Her interdisciplinary research integrates African Diaspora literature; African, American, and African American studies; and Black Feminist/Womanist theory and criticism. She has published articles in the *Western Journal of Black Studies, a/b: Auto/Biography Studies, bma/Sonia Sanchez Literary Review*, as well as review essays for *Legacy* and *Early American Literature*. Her book, *The Black Aesthetic Unbound: Theorizing the Dilemma of Self and Identity in Eighteenth-Century African American Literature* (Ohio State University Press, 2008), explores the culturally specific African origins of the eighteenth-century

Afro-British American literary and cultural self through a conceptualization of the dilemma posed by competing African, American, and British cultural identities. Her current project *#earlyBlack ChristianWomensLivesMatter: Spirituality and Social Justice Movements in Eighteenth- and Nineteenth-Century America* explores intersecting themes of religion and politics through the diverse Black women's texts and genres—sermon, poetry, and epistle. Additional book projects include *Looking for Phillis*, an in-depth study on the Senegambian poetics and oral traditions that influence the poetry of Phillis Wheatley, as well as a study on Anna Julia Cooper, race, gender, and double consciousness. She is also a Phi Beta Kappa member, 2001 AAUW fellow, and a 2003–2005 Postdoctoral Fellow in African and Afro-American Studies at Washington University in St. Louis.

JANAKA B. LEWIS, PHD, is Director of the Center for the Study of the New South and Associate Professor in the Department of English at the University of North Carolina at Charlotte. Her areas of research interest include African American literature of the nineteenth century (specifically narrative studies) and African American women's writing. She has worked on publications about Black women and mobility as portrayed through literature in the nineteenth century and representations of motherhood in post-emancipation African American literature. She is the author of over a dozen articles on Black women's writing and was recognized as the inaugural Ruth B. Shaw Humanities Scholar at UNC Charlotte.

THERESA RAJACK-TALLEY, PHD, is Professor in Pan-African Studies and Vice Provost of Equity and Inclusion at Dalhousie University, Nova Scotia, Canada. Rajack-Talley spent much of her career in the Department of Pan-African Studies at the University of Louisville and earned her PhD in sociology at the University of Kentucky. Her academic work has focused on the intersectionality of social inequality, gender equity, race/ethnicity, racism, and social justice issues in low-resource households and communities in North America, the Caribbean, and the African diaspora. She has taught courses on racism and sexism, global poverty, and Pan-Africanism and has published many refereed articles on related themes, as well as two books—*Poverty Is a Person: Human Agency, Women and Caribbean Households* (Ian Randle Publishers, 2016) and *Living Racism: Through the Barrel of the Book* (Lexington Books, 2017)—with a forthcoming co-edited volume titled *Beyond the Kitchen Table: Black Women and Global Food Systems*. She has been a Fulbright Scholar and has been recognized by the Kentucky Senate for her leadership in education, research, and service to the community. Prior to her position at Dalhousie University, she developed and led a PhD in Pan-African Studies and a robust diversity plan as Associate Dean at the University of Louisville's College of Arts and Sciences.

TRACY SHARPLEY-WHITING, PHD, is the Gertrude Conaway Vanderbilt Distinguished Professor of Humanities (AADS and French) and Vice Provost for Arts and Libraries at Vanderbilt University, where she also directs the Callie House Research Center. She is co-chair of the Chair at the Table project. Sharpley-Whiting is the former Associate Provost of Academic Advancement and Chair of the Department of African American and Diaspora Studies at Vanderbilt University. She is the author, editor, or co-editor of fifteen books, including *Bricktop's Paris: African American Women in Paris between the Two World Wars* and *The Autobiography of Ada Bricktop Smith, or Miss Baker Regrets* (SUNY Press, 2015, two volumes) and *Pimps Up, Ho's Down: Hip-Hop's Hold on Young Black Women* (New York University Press, 2008). She is co-editor of the *Norton Anthology of Theory and Criticism*, senior co-editor of the journal *Palimpsest*, one of the series editors of *Blacks in the Diaspora* (Indiana University Press, 2007–2015), and co-series editor of *Philosophy and Race* (SUNY Press). She served on the Executive Council of the Modern Language Association from 2014 to 2018.

STEPHANIE SHONEKAN, PHD, is Dean of the College of Arts and Humanities and Professor of Ethnomusicology at the University of Maryland, College Park. In 2003, she earned a PhD in ethnomusicology and folklore with a minor in African American Studies from Indiana University. From 2003 to 2011, she taught at Columbia College Chicago, and from 2011 to 2018, she was a faculty member at the University of Missouri in the Black Studies Department and the School of Music. From 2015 to 2018, she was chair of the Department of Black Studies at the University of Missouri. From 2018 to 2020, she was professor and chair of the W. E. B. Du Bois Department of Afro-American Studies at the University of Massachusetts Amherst. From 2020 to 2022, she was Senior Associate Dean of the College of Arts and Science and Professor of Music at the University of Missouri. Shonekan's dual heritage in West Africa and the West Indies allows her to straddle the Black world comfortably. She has published articles on afrobeat and Fela Kuti, as well as American and Nigerian hip-hop, and American country music. Her publications explore the nexus where identity, history, culture, and music meet. Her books include *The Life of Camilla Williams, African American Classical Singer and Opera Diva* (Edwin Mellen Press, 2011); *Soul, Country, and the USA: Race and Identity in American Music Culture* (Palgrave Macmillan, 2015); *Black Lives Matter & Music* (Indiana University Press, 2018); and *Black Resistance in the Americas* (Routledge, 2018).

COLETTE M. TAYLOR, EDD, is Professor in Educational and Organizational Learning and Leadership; Special Assistant to the Provost for Strategic Directions; and Director of the Center for Social Transformation and Leadership at Seattle University. Prior to her current role, Dr. Taylor served as a department chair for two years and a doctoral program director for five years at Seattle University. She has accumulated over twenty-nine years of professional higher education and leadership experience at Seattle University, Texas Tech University, Middle Tennessee State University, University of Florida, Nova Southeastern University, and Wake Forest University. She is a past president of the Southern Association of College Student Affairs and has served on the editorial boards of the *College Student Affairs Journal*, *Journal for Diversity in Higher Education*, and *Journal of Student Affairs Research and Practice*. In addition, she is an active member of the International Leadership Association, American College Personnel Association, Association for the Study of Higher Education (ASHE), Engagement Scholarship Consortium, and Student Affairs Administrators in Higher Education (NASPA). Dr. Taylor's teaching, scholarship, and service is multicultural and multicontextual in nature and situated in the fields of leadership, social justice, and education.

Index

AAUP, 69

AAUW, 69

academic achievement, 86

academic freedom, 77

academic integrity, 124

Academic Program Portfolio Review, 142

academic programs, 142

access, equity, and diversity (AED), 49

accessibility, 122

accountability, 13, 62, 99, 114, 115, 126, 140; partners, 112

activism, 75

Adams, Stephanie, ix, 9, 26, 30–33

administration, 3–4; administration 101, 3; top-down, 10

administrative goals, 65

advice, 58

advocate, 24, 49, 80, 116, 126, 130, 137

AED. *See* access, equity, and diversity

affirmative action, 124

Africa, 29, 120

African Burial Ground, 87

African Feminist Values, 15. *See also* communal care; self-care

African Nova Scotians, 121

age, x, 79

aggressions, 64, 93, 130

Aid for Families with Dependent Children (AFDC), 112

allies/allyship, 64, 65, 103, 127, 129, 130, 131

alumni development opportunities, 77

American Council on Education: Women of Color conference, 32

Angelou, Maya, xiii, 18, 88

angry Black woman, 96

anti-Black racism, 103

anti-Semitism, 123

anxiety, 144

Arbery, Ahmaud, 114

ASALH, 69

ask questions, 153

assimilation, 124

Association of Governing Boards, 148, 154

attribution, 98

authentic self, 116

Babyface, 27
balance, 3, 4–6, 14, 22, 28
Baldwin, James, 25, 157
Barber, William J., 52
Beckles, Hilary, 133
Bennett College, 25
best practices, 17
Bethune, Mary McLeod, 2, 25, 113
bias, 112, 129, 150
Binders Full of Black Women and Black Nonbinary People in Academia, 48
Black, Indigenous, and people of color (BIPOC), 49
Black box, 102
Black Faculty and Staff Caucus, 125
Black girl magic, xii
Black in the Ivory Tower: #BlackInTheIvoryTower, 48; *Black Women in the Ivory Tower, 1850–1954: An Intellectual History*, 25, 65, 69, 89, 118, 162; *Telling Histories: Black Women Historians in the Ivory Tower*, 25, 89
Black Lives Matter, 49, 125
Black Maledom, 95, 96
Black matriarchal superwomen, 124
Black motherhood in academia, 72, 81
Black Power, 77
Black Studies, 3, 125, 158; and Black Studies Research, 125
Black Superwoman, 138

Black tax, 106
Black Women's Mental Health: Balancing Strength and Vulnerability, 162
Black Women's Studies Booklist, 132, 162
board of trustees, 15, 142, 147–155; managing up, 153
body autonomy, 94
boss mentality, 18–19
Bowman, Joye, 28
Bracey, John H., Jr., 13
branding, 149, 154
Brock, Lisa, 27
Brooks, Rayshard, 114
Bryant, Martina, 73
budget process, 4, 13, 35, 43, 61, 76, 81, 131, 151; faculty, 81
build bridges, 64, 116, 130
bullying, 96, 98, 122
BWSA, 69

campus caucuses, 125
campus safety, 151
Canada, 3, 121, 125–126
capacity building, 123
care, 38
care work, 104
career trajectory, 67
Carew, Jan, 132
Caribbean, 29, 120
chair: activism, 7, 75, 120; books, 17; cohorts, 50, 69; forward facing, 13; misrepresented/disrespected, 12; pipeline, 46
Chair at the Table, 3–7, 11, 23, 38, 69, 122, 127;

peer-mentoring network,
    21, 69
change, 3, 6–7, 15, 75, 115, 116,
    126, 130; agent, 116, 117
Chief Diversity Officer (CDO),
    111–115
Chisholm, Shirley, 113
Chronicle of Higher Education, 15
citing Black women, 65
citizenship, 91; of feelings, 92,
    93, 96, 97, 98
civil rights movement, 77
CLA, 69
classism, 121
cliques, 19
coach, 19
coalition, 131
cognitive dissonance, 144
cohorts, 65
Cole, Johnnetta Betsch, ix–xiii,
    17, 20, 113
collaboration, xii, 15, 72, 82, 112,
    115, 125, 131, 144
collaborative leadership
    style, 20
collective care, 18
collective histories, 29
colonialism, 120, 121, 122, 125,
    131
colonization, 132
Color Purple, The, 43–44, 47,
    48, 53
Combahee River Collective, 96
communal care, 15
community, 3, 7, 18, 77, 126,
    131; building, 18, 62–63, 74,
    123

community colleges, 79–89;
    budgets, 84; funding, 81–82;
    older students, 80
compassion, 15
compromise, self, 143, 144
confidentially, 19
conflict management, 63, 75,
    130, 132; resolution, 63, 75
conversations, 114, 117; "off the
    record," 17
Cooper, Anna Julia, 2, 25, 65,
    77, 113
Cooper, Brittney, 66
Coppin, Fanny Jackson, 113
courses, 82; assessments, 84;
    cross listed, 58, 59
COVID-19, 4, 5, 7, 37, 50, 76,
    114
create new opportunities, 130
critical race theory, 152
Crunkfeminists, 66, 94
cultural discrimination, 121
cultural identity, 24
cultural taxation, 104
CUPA-HR, 97

damsel in distress, 128, 129
Davis, Angela, 15
Dean's Administrative
    Council, 73
deanships, 158
decision-making, 82
decolonization, 123
DEI (diversity, equity, and
    inclusion), 3, 6–7, 8, 49, 62,
    63, 112, 113, 114, 116, 117
Department Chair, The, 16, 34, 46

department chair: accountability, 62; advocate, 24, 49, 116, 130, 137; balancing day and evening courses, 82; balancing student, faculty, and administration needs, 137, 142; balancing student enrollment and faculty research, 61, 84; budgeting, 76, 78, 81, 82, 84, 137, 142; chair-faculty relationships, 142; challenges, 61; climate, 75; collaboration, 72; curriculum, 61, 71, 76, 78, 123, 137; duties, 43; educate, 130; funding, 71, 76, 77, 81, 82; goals, 68; grants, 77; job description, 34–37; organize, 19; policy, 17, 75; politics, 71, 140; programming, 61, 76; references, 51; research, 61; responsibilities, 61, 68; rewards, 61; role of, 17, 38, 137; stability, 98; staffing, 71, 76; standards, 17, 63, 140; strategic plans, 17, 68; tasks and skills, 46; transparency, 63; trust, 72
department policies, 43, 75
Diaspora, 29, 120
dictator, 21
Difficult Dialogues training, 64
dignity, 142, 143, 144
disabilities, x, 20
disaggregated data, 125
disciplines, working across, 81, 82, 86, 131

discrimination, x, 104, 112, 120, 121, 123, 126
disempowering, 131
disenfranchisement, 121
divergent learners, 20
diverse identities, 131
diverse student population, 84
diversification, 130
diversity, 15, 34, 80, 103, 104, 112, 114, 115, 116, 122, 123, 124, 130, 131
diversity, equity, and inclusion. *See* DEI
diversity statement, 98
document your work, 18
Du Bois, W. E. B., 2

East India, 120
economic crisis, 37
ecosystem, 113
emails, 16, 18
emotional labor, 104
empathize, 14, 19, 144
engagement, 143; with community, 131
enrollment, 151
epistolary writing, 10
equitable, 20, 92, 114, 116
equity, 63, 82, 106, 112, 114, 115, 116, 122, 123, 124, 130
equity, diversity, inclusion, and accessibility (EDIA), 123, 125, 126, 132
equity minded, 113
erased, 26, 139, 140
estimated family contribution (EFC), 151

ethical, 20, 82, 92
ethics: humane, 17;
   professional, 17
ethnicity, 95, 125
Eurocentrism, 120, 122, 131
evaluating colleagues, 51, 129
Evans, Stephanie, 9, 10, 13–25,
   26, 28, 37, 46, 65, 95, 98
exercise, 23
experiential learning
   opportunities, 83

Facebook, 48
facilitate, 130
faculty, 7, 86, 88; assessments, 84;
   assignments, 85; departures,
   97, 98; evaluations, 51, 129;
   faculty councils, 63; faculty
   handbook, 43; full time, 77;
   intercampus faculty cabinets,
   63; junior, 14; leadership, 98;
   lines, 51; part time, 77, 85;
   promotion, 98; publishing,
   84; research, 84; retention, 98;
   senior, 14, 77; service, 84
failure, 124, 125, 160
fairness, 20
faith, 20, 24, 136, 144, 151
families, 30, 65
feelings, 93, 96, 97, 98
female networks, 15
feminism, 92, 94, 96
Feminist Wire, 74
Floyd, George, 47, 49, 103, 114,
   126
focus, 1, 160
focus day, 16

foremothers, 65
forgiveness, 140, 141
fortitude, 116
funding, 71, 81, 104, 151

Gay, Claudine, 1–2
gender, 27, 95
gender bias, 62
gender identity, 120, 125
gender politics, 6
gender studies/research, 34, 71
generational wealth, 114
goals, 65, 66, 67; aspirational,
   117, 124, 138; department,
   68, 75; hoped for, 117;
   inspirational, 124; legacy, 117;
   team centered, 142
grace, 88, 116
gratitude, 38, 141
Grimke, Charlotte Forten, 77
GRIT (Grace, Resilience,
   Intuitive Intellectual
   Capacity, and Tonality), 116
group meetings, 19
growth, 18
growth mindset, 117
gun violence, 151

Haitian immigrants, 104
Hamad, Ruby, 128, 129
Hamer, Fannie Lou, 132
Hannah-Jones, Nikole, 15, 49,
   52, 105, 106
Harlem, 87
harm reduction, 91
Harper, Frances Ellen Watkins,
   76, 128

Harris, Carla, 149
healing: communal, 59; personal, 59
health, 22, 66, 98, 125, 138
hearing, perspective based, 64
Hensley, Chiara, 147
HERS Leadership Institute, 102
herstory, 57, 65
Hispanic-Serving Institutions, x
historical values, 25
historical wellness, 15
Historically Black Colleges and Universities (HBCUs), x, 82
holistic evaluations, 89
Holness, Andrew, 62
homophobia, 121, 123
Ho'oponopono, 140, 141, 145
Houston, Whitney, 27, 28
HUGs (historically underrepresented and underserved groups), 115
human rights, 120, 132
humanities programs, 81
humanity, 19, 112, 116, 141–143
humility, xi, 17, 50–51, 135, 142, 144, 145
Hurston, Zora Neale, 44

identity matters, 92, 93
immigrant, 122
imposter syndrome, 32
inclusion, 104, 112, 114, 115, 117; inclusive community, 116; inclusive leadership style, 84, 144; inclusiveness, 25, 122, 123, 130; statements, 98

indentureship, 120
Indigenous communities, 121, 123, 126, 131
inequality, 112, 113, 114, 120, 121, 125, 129; admissions process, 113; classroom experience, 113; curricula development, 113; racial, 120; scholarly evaluation, 113
inhumaneness, 112
inner peace, 18
institutional analysis, 125
institutional colonization, 132
institutional environment, 23
institutional memory, 49, 50
institutional resources, 114
institutional support, 114
institutions, identity, 98
integrity, 96, 113, 115
intellectualism, 119
intercampus faculty cabinets, 63
interdisciplinary, 57, 158
intergenerational communication, 10
internships, 83
interpersonal dynamics, 51
intersectionality, racial/sexual, 15, 120, 125, 132, 145, 166
Islamophobia, 123

Jacobs, Harriet, 157
Jenkins, Barry, 25
Jim Crow, xi, 128
Jim Crow Guide, 127
job market, 83
joy, 51
justice, 96, 112, 115

kindness, 38
King, Martin Luther, Jr., 157

labor contracts, 151
Laney, Lucy Craft, 77
Langley, April, 27
language, respectful, 140
leader humility, 141–143
leadership, 4–6, 15, 37, 84, 98, 102, 141–144; board of trustees, 149, 154–155; collaborative, 20; identity, 99; inclusiveness, 25; intellect and critical analysis, 125; moral responsibility, 25; radical, 77; senior leadership, 104, 107, 126, 130, 159; servant, 88; skills, 116, 121, 125; training, 22; transformative, 117
learn, 24; learning, x; learning from yourself, 33
Lee, Butch, 124
legacy, 116
letter-as-essay, 10
liberatory action, 98
lifelong learning, 33, 117
lifting as we climb, 15, 130
listening to others, 64, 69, 78, 116; students, 157
loan debt, 112
Lorde, Audre, xii, 66, 92, 98
love, 141, 145
Loveland, Trish, 28
low-performing programs, 82

Makeba, Miriam, 29
Malcolm X, 132

male superiority, 95, 125, 139
managing up, 51, 153
Mandela, Nelson, 29
manuals, 17, 76
marginalization, x, 20, 34, 96, 98, 99, 104, 126, 131, 139, 140
Marley, Bob, 91
masking, 48
McBride, Dwight, 117
meditate, 23
Mellon Mays Graduate Initiatives Program (MMGIP), 74
Mellon Mays Undergraduate Fellowship (MMUF), 74, 104, 105
mental health, 14, 15, 18, 23, 89, 125, 128, 138; practices, 15, 23–24, 89
menteeship, 26, 69
mentor network, 32
mentorship, xii, 3, 21, 26, 69, 71, 72, 77, 84, 101, 103, 105, 121, 122, 127, 130, 131, 132, 157
microaggressions, 93, 139
Mi'kma'ki, 121
mindful listening, 116
mindfulness, 88
mission statements, 96, 97
mission-critical, 137
Monae, Janelle, 92
moral responsibility, 25
Morrison, Toni, 15, 18
motivation, 67
multidimensional perspective, 153
multiple identities, 139

National Association of Colored Women, 15

National Center for Education Statistics, 97

National Charter on Anti-Black Racism and Black Inclusion, 126

National Dialogue on Anti-Black Racism, 126

National Women's Studies Association, 71

negative feelings, 141

negative stereotypes, 124

nepotism, 19

network(s), 18, 19, 20, 23, 28, 29, 69, 74, 76

nicety (nice nasty), 20

Nicol, Donna, 21

novels, gender-based violence in, 105

Obama, Barack, 86

Oh, Sandra, 12

old boy network, 127

older students, problems of, 80, 86

online learning, 80, 84

open office hours, 16

oppressions, 26, 77, 96, 120, 126; race-gender, 98, 138

organizational balance, 28, 142

organizational leader, 19, 105, 124, 141

organize, 19, 65, 66, 99

Orisha Oya, 93–94

Palimpsest, 8–9, 15, 38, 124, 131, 134, 167

pandemic, 4, 22, 50, 72, 74, 76, 88, 114, 143; effects on academia, 72

parenting, 74

partnerships, 131

passion, 30–31, 32, 117

patriarchal tendencies, 95, 103, 122, 131

Pearce, Tola, 27

pearls, 115

pedagogies, 123

peer mentoring, 3, 20, 21, 122, 158

peer observations, 45

peer relationships, 24

Peña, Lorgia Garcia, 105

personal histories, 29

personal leadership philosophy, 138

personal needs, 60

personal values, 144

personality management, 151

Phillips, Bum, 33

Pierce-Baker, Charlotte, 73

Player, Willa, 25

pleasure, 66

policies, 43, 75; policy, 81, 123

political crisis, 37; dynamics, 140; politics, ix, 75, 140

power structure, 103

predominantly white institutions (PWIs), x, 34, 74, 104, 106

problem-solving strategies, 19, 81, 160

professional archive, 18

professional development, 86, 88

professor of color, 45

provost-level appointments, 158
public health crisis, 37
public history/historian, 85–87
purpose, 117

queer people, 20, 77, 78
Queer Studies, 125

race, 27, 95, 125; identity, 129; studies/research, 34
race, class, gender, 63, 120, 125, 127
race and gender, x, 14, 34, 106; intersection of, 132, 139; oppression, 98; race-gender tax, 98
racial crisis, 37
racial dynamics, 140
racial etiquette, 127, 129
racial family, 96
racial fatigue, 114
racial inequality, 120
racial justice/injustice, 103, 104
racialization, 120, 122, 128
racialized female, 120, 122, 128, 129, 130, 132
racism, 97, 103, 112, 121, 123, 125, 126, 138, 139; white women and, 128
racist-sexist stereotypes, 24
radical leadership, 77
radicalized females, 119, 120, 121, 122, 124, 126, 127, 133
Rae, Issa, 91
RCM (responsibility-centered management), 6
reading across disciplines, 57, 62

Reagon, Bernice Johnson, 15
recognition, 106, 107
recruitment, 37, 72, 106; of faculty, 123
religion, x
remote work, 88, 89, 114
reparation, 141
research: tenure-track, 14; what you love, 18
resiliency, 116, 160
resistance, 96, 130, 138
resources, 34, 65, 68
responsibilities, 68, 116
restorative justice, 91, 112
results-driven outcomes, 115
retention, 98, 106, 143
risk, 144
roles, 12, 13, 119; of white women, 127
RTP (reappointment, tenure, post-tenure review), 51

sacred self, 92, 93, 94, 95, 96
safe space, 123; training, 62
scholarly credentials, 158
Schomburg Center for Research in Black Culture, 87
SEEDs (Sister Educators Eating Dinner(s)), 73, 74
self-actualization, 91, 94
self-care, xii, 15, 16, 18, 22, 33, 66, 76, 77, 78, 88, 89, 115, 137
self-compassion, 16
self-defeating attitudes/thinking, 152, 153
self-development, 3, 4–6

self-governance, 94
self-importance, 144
self-naming, 94–95
self-preservation, 48, 66, 112
self-reflection, 96
self-reliance, 15, 18
self-worth, 144
"semi-presences," 48
senior leadership, 159
senior scholar, 76, 77
servant leadership, 88
service, 84, 88, 105
sexism, 121, 123, 124, 139
sexual orientation, x
shadowing, 149
Shange, Ntozoke, 95, 96
Sharpley-Whiting, Tracy, 7–9
Shonekan, Stephanie, 9, 25–30
silence, 48, 49
Simmons, Ruth, 2, 113
Simone, Nina, 29
single representation, 15
Sirleaf, Ellen Johnson, xii
sistah-doctah, 60
sista-scholars, xii, 28, 30, 43, 46, 74, 76, 77
sister-administrator, xii
sister-director, 71
sister-friends, 47
sisterhood, 26, 27, 28, 71, 72, 73, 99, 111
situational awareness, 144
slavery, 120
Smith, Malinda, 122
social activism, 115, 120
social class, 120, 121
social identity, 139

social inequities, 120, 121
social justice/injustice, 59, 62, 103, 112, 120, 121, 125, 126, 132, 140
social media, 48
social mobility, 112
social obligation, 122
social stratification, 120, 121
social support system, 23
social transformation, 121
Solange, 11
soul work, 116
South Africa, 29
Speak Truth to Power forum, 126
spill-outs, 48
spiritual woundedness, 114
St. Theresa's Prayer, 135
staffing, 7, 71
Standard Operating Procedure, 76
Staples, Robert, 95, 96
STEM, 81
stereotypes, 124, 128
strategize, 19, 65, 127
stress, 14, 92, 137, 142
Strong Black Woman (SBW), 138
structural/systemic "isms," 123
struggle, 116
students, 7, 15, 155–156; academic freedom for, 77; activism, 7; advocate for, 81; divergent, 20; Indigenous, 123; loan debt, 112; marginalized, 20, 104; student surveys, 81; success, 88, 123; underrepresented, 123

succession plan, 22, 149

support, 24, 28, 38, 68, 155;
    institutional, 157

surveys, 20, 21, 68, 81

survival strategies, 15

SWOT (strengths, weaknesses,
    opportunities, threats), 21

sycophants, 21

Talley, Clarence, 132

Taylor, Breonna, 114

Taylor, Colette, 17

teaching design, 123

teaching skills, 86

team-centered attitude, 143

technological innovations, 77,
    84, 86

tenure, 44; denial of, 106

Terborg-Penn, Rosalyn, 15

Terry, Esther, 28

therapy, 66

third reconstruction, 52

"Thulasizwe," 29

time management, 16

timing, 67, 68, 78

Title IX, 151

tokenism, 15, 124

tonality, 116

toxic culture, 140

training, 68

transformation, 3, 6–7, 116, 117

transgendered people, 20, 77, 78

transparency, 20, 63, 82, 85, 92,
    131

tribal colleges, x

Trinidad/Tobago, 120

trust, 24, 52, 65, 72, 115, 155

Trusteeship Magazine, 154

"Truth & Reconciliation
    Commission of Canada:
    Calls for Action Report,"
    125–126

truth-telling, 20, 144

T/TT faculty (tenure/tenure
    track), 7, 14, 44, 45, 51, 57, 74

Tubman, Harriet, 124, 132

unions, 18, 36; Black Student
    Union, 49, 54

United Nations, 87

university concerns, 74; culture,
    17; documents, 68; strategic
    plans, 17, 68

vice provost, 123

violence, 105, 151

vision, 78; educational, 115;
    statement, 96

visionaries, 113

Walker, Alice, 43–44, 53

Wallace, Michele, 95, 96

Washington, Albert "Nuh," 133

well-being, 33, 66, 75, 78

wellness, 14, 22–24, 37, 63, 74,
    76, 77, 98, 133

white patriarchy, 124, 129

white privilege, ix, 125, 128, 130,
    131

white supremacy, 29, 44, 95

white syndrome (mini-me), 130

white tears, 129

white women, 127–129, 140; as
    damsels in distress, 128, 129

Winans, Cece, 27, 28
wisdom, 111, 115, 117
Women and Gender Studies, 77, 125
women of African descent, 29
women of color (WOC), 49
Women's Studies, 3
workforce development, 80
workforce-related jobs, 83

work-life balance, 18, 28, 32
Wright, Marion Thompson, 25
write, 18
writing support, 74
"writing to live" symposium, 74
written communication, 18; documentation, 16

Zephir, Flore, 27